THE ELIJAH PEOPLE

by

Roger Aubrey

**Grosvenor House
Publishing Limited**

This book is published by
Grosvenor House Publishing Ltd
28-30 High Street, Guildford, Surrey, GU1 3EL.
www.grosvenorhousepublishing.co.uk

A CIP record for this book
is available from the British Library

ISBN 978-1-78148-758-7

Also by Roger Aubrey

The Circle of Life
Discovering God
Stars and Sand
Angels

About the Author

Roger Aubrey was born and raised in Cardiff, Wales. He lives in the city with his wife Dianne. He has been a Christian since 1966. Roger serves on the leadership team of All Nations Church, with responsibility for teaching and preaching. He enjoys cricket and rugby, and visits Churches and Bible Colleges throughout the world, teaching the Word of God and building up the Body of Christ. Roger has a Master's Degree and a PhD in Christian Theology from Cardiff University. He likes to read biographies of those who shape history.

For Tabitha and Ezra
May you see His coming

Contents

Foreword

What makes the prophet Elijah such a notable character in the Bible? What is 'the spirit and power of Elijah' by which John the Baptist ministered? Why is Elijah so closely linked to the coming of our Lord Jesus Christ? And what does all this have to do with you and me?

At a time when the Church seems to be 'blown here and there by every wind of teaching' it is refreshingly reassuring to find a book so thoroughly Biblical in its content, Christ honouring in its presentation and helpfully practical in its application. The Elijah people, we discover, are not some elite company of super-saints ready to be revealed at the moment of crisis, nor are they an end-time manifestation of Old Testament ministries. They are, rather, the Church – the whole Church – endued with power from on high and totally committed to serving the purpose of God in the earth.

There is nothing novel or titillating in Dr Aubrey's teaching. It will not tickle the ears nor stir desire for mystery of those who 'spend all their time doing nothing but talking about and listening to the latest ideas'. This is not another theory, yet another obscure concept, nor even a weary intellectual exercise. This book has a punch and a bite – it makes radical demands that are impossible to ignore. This book, I say, is radical. It does not take us off on flights of fancy, but leads us back to the very roots and foundations of Biblical Christianity. It shows the

Church (however dark the world) not as victim but victor; not as the impassive observer of unstoppable events, but as the inspired overcomer of every situation. It tells you who you are – a child of God; what we are – the Church of Christ; and why we are here as God's Elijah people. It exhorts us to power, prayer and prophecy.

Those who are familiar with the ministry of Roger Aubrey and have been blessed by his insights and teaching will not find this work wanting. New readers will be equally blessed.

In many ways this is the book I wish I had written. But then, if I had, you would not have this, much better book in your hands now.

Tony Ling
February 2012

Preface

I first became aware of the biblical concept of the Elijah People during the 1980s in the pages of *Restoration* magazine, published by Harvestime. This ground-breaking publication was the prophetic voice of men like Bryn Jones and Arthur Wallis, who were the pioneers of God's restoration purpose in the mid and late twentieth century. Through these spiritual giants I was introduced to the ministry and message of other major men of God, such as Ern Baxter, DeVern Fromke, Tony Ling and E. Stanley Jones, all of whom have played a significant part in extending the kingdom of God in many nations of the world.

From the very first time I heard of the Elijah People I was transfixed and captured by its truth: that before Jesus returns to this earth in glory, Elijah will come and will restore all things, just as Jesus promised. This Elijah is a corporate Elijah, the Church triumphant and glorious, the spotless Bride of Christ, the fully-grown Body of Christ.

The manifestation of the Church as the Elijah People is desperately needed today. The Church must recapture its prophetic, radical voice and so qualify to be a people worthy of the name of Jesus, and in doing so hasten his coming. We live at the climax of history when the Church is destined to reach maturity. We have to be honest: there is still a considerable way to go before that maturity is achieved. The original Elijah and the second

Elijah, John the Baptist, both encountered societies and spiritual environments that had largely forsaken the living God. The time has now come in our day for the voice and life of God to be heard and witnessed in a dimension the world has not yet seen. That is the tremendous responsibility of the Elijah People: to speak for and represent God to this world as his restorers.

There is an enormous personal cost involved when one belongs to the Elijah People. Elijah himself had many enemies and intense opposition. He sometimes stood alone as the prophet of God, while those he confronted tried to destroy him. His integrity and character were impugned; his words were twisted and questioned; his life was constantly in danger. He was persecuted and was the object of misunderstanding, scorn and raw hatred. John the Baptist too paid a massive price for his revelation of God's purpose and his identity as the second Elijah. In fact, he paid the ultimate price: he was imprisoned and murdered. Despite this, both Elijah and John were captured by a vision and a message to establish God's status quo. For them, the price they were willing to pay to see that vision realised and to ensure their message from God was heard was worth it.

At certain points this book is not a comfortable read; I have to confess it was not a comfortable book to write. Nevertheless, I am convinced it is a book that needed to be written; and I offer it as something that should be read by those who are serious about being authentic disciples of Jesus Christ.

I should like to thank the following people for their invaluable help: Ann Sneddon, for the artwork and cover design; Tony Ling, for reading the manuscript and for doing me the immense honour of writing the foreword; and Dr. James Aubrey, my editor, whose insight and patient determination made a significant contribution to the production and content of this book. Finally, thanks to my wife Dianne, for giving me time and space to pursue the task. I hope it was worth it.

RA
Christmas 2011

Author's Note

The reader will notice that I have replaced the term *the LORD* in the Old Testament scriptures quoted in the book with the name Yahweh, which is the original Hebrew word that *the LORD* translates. Yahweh is the name of God that he has revealed to us in the Old Testament. It is his personal, covenant name. Yahweh sounds like the Hebrew phrase 'he is', hence God calls himself I AM WHO I AM. In John 8:58 Jesus declared himself to be Yahweh when he said, "Before Abraham was born, I am!" Yahweh describes God as the self-existent, self-sufficient, unchanging God. He is the infinite God who is before time, outside of time and above time. My reason for using the actual name rather than the traditional term *the LORD* is because Elijah's name means *Yahweh is my God*. I trust it will also assist the reader in appreciating familiar verses in a new way.

INTRODUCTION

I'll be back!

Jesus is coming back! The awesome truth of this simple statement has been the steadfast hope and continued conviction of the Church ever since the Lord Jesus Christ rose victorious from the dead and ascended into heaven two thousand years ago. The true Church always lives in the light of his coming. The Bible closes with the anticipating cry of the Holy Spirit and the Church: *"Come, Lord Jesus"* (Revelation 22:17-20). Jesus himself promised that he will come again:

"If I go and prepare a place for you, I will come back and take you to be with me, that you also may be where I am." (John 14:3)

Even as Jesus ascended into heaven and his disciples gazed upwards in awe and wonder as he went, two angels came alongside them to remind them, and to declare to us, that one day he will return:

"This same Jesus, who has been taken from you into heaven, will come back in the same way you have seen him go into heaven." (Acts 1:11)

The rest of the New Testament is filled with references to the incontrovertible fact that one day the Lord Jesus

Christ will leave his throne in heaven and return to this earth again. He will not be born in a stable in Bethlehem as he was in his first coming; he will come in all his majestic glory as King of kings and Lord of lords, as the Judge of all mankind. Jesus' Second Coming will conclude earthly human history and usher in the age to come. The Church, therefore, should constantly focus on Jesus' promise that he will come again. We must not doubt it, nor dare ignore it. The Second Coming of Jesus must never be relegated to a postscript or an occasional sermon. It should be paramount in our thinking and a means of constant encouragement and challenge for us. It should guide our every decision. The Second Coming of Jesus is the fuel that fires the Church. Peter warned of scoffers who would doubt the words of Jesus (2Peter 3:3-4) and call into question his coming. He reminded his readers that:

The day of the Lord will come like a thief. The heavens will disappear with a roar; the elements will be destroyed by fire: and the earth and everything in it will be laid bare. (2Peter 3:10)

When will Jesus come back?

Tragically, this question, which should be a matter of joy, excitement and anticipation for all Christians, has caused the Church and, more importantly, the testimony of Jesus, more aggravation and confusion than almost any other aspect of Christianity. I do not wish to add fuel to that particular fire, nor waste time and space going over tired and futile arguments. Far too often Christians furiously debate what they think are the important details and minutiae of the Second Coming and end up missing the bigger, more significant, picture. Many people wrongly read the book of Revelation that way. Therefore, this particular book is not an examination of the end times; you will not find in these pages explanations of the millennium (Revelation 20), the beast (Revelation 13), and the four horsemen (Revelation 6), important as they are. Rather, this book is all about a people, a people who will speed the Day of Jesus' coming (2Peter 3:11-12). I call them the Elijah People and it is my conviction that there is a strong biblical basis to justify such a description. I believe that the Elijah People are the true Church, the kingdom people of God. I am convinced that the maturity and spiritual condition of the Church as the Elijah People are directly related to the timing of Jesus' coming. As the primary agent of the kingdom of God on earth, the Church has a unique role to play in God's eternal purpose in Christ. The Church is the Body of Christ and the Bride of Christ (1Corinthians 12:12-31; Revelation 21:2-11; 22:17). As the Bride of Christ, the Church's responsibility is to make herself ready for the coming of her Bridegroom (Revelation 19:7-8). When she has done so, he will come. As the Body of Christ, the Church must grow to maturity (Ephesians 4:13), to represent fully on earth its Head who sits on his heavenly throne. When the Body is fully mature its Head will come.

Most of the debates about the coming of Jesus mystifyingly overlook an important passage in Acts, when Peter preached to the crowds after the crippled man was miraculously healed. Peter specifically answered the question concerning when Jesus will come again:

"Repent and turn again, so that your sins may be wiped away, in order that times of refreshing may

> *come from the presence of the Lord; and that He*
> *may send Jesus, the Christ appointed for you,*
> *whom heaven must receive until the times of the*
> *restoration of all things about which God spoke*
> *by the mouth of His holy prophets from ancient*
> *time." (Acts 3:19-21)*

There is the simple answer to our question: Jesus must remain in heaven until the restoration of all things spoken by the prophets. He cannot and will not return to earth until something has happened: the restoration of all things spoken by the Old Testament prophets. In the following chapters I aim to explain what this means. We will begin by examining the term *restoration*. Then we will explore this phrase 'spoken by the prophets', and concentrate on one of the major Old Testament prophets who features in the New Testament and is mentioned specifically in reference to the restoration of all things: Elijah. Then we will bring these two strands together to see that the Church, the Elijah People that gives this book its title, are those who will restore all things and hasten the coming of Jesus.

Qualities and mission

It is true that the biblical image of the Elijah People does not tell us all there is to know about the Church and the kingdom of God. None of the biblical images of the Church and kingdom of God does that on its own; the Church is a multi-faceted expression of an infinite God, and we must be familiar with each of these images if we are to appreciate the nature, purpose and glorious future of the Church. The description of the Church as the Elijah People, however, does give us particularly specific, important insights into the nature of the Church as it expresses the kingdom of God. It also reveals to us something of what the Church has yet to become in God's restoration purpose in order to see the Lord Jesus Christ return in glory.

This book is not a classical character study of the lives of Elijah and John the Baptist (the second Elijah), who will also feature significantly in these pages. Instead, I will discuss examples and instances from their lives and ministries to demonstrate the kind of people we are as the Elijah People. Primarily, therefore, I am concerned about the qualities of the Elijah People rather than emphasising our mission. That is not because mission is secondary or unimportant; of course it is immensely vital. Elijah, John the Baptist and the Church were, and are, all 'sent' by God. Indeed, I shall touch on the mission of the Elijah People in the chapter *Turning Hearts*. I agree that ultimately we cannot separate the nature of the Church from its mission. I am particularly indebted to the work of Christopher Wright in this regard, and would recommend highly his excellent book *The Mission of God*. Nevertheless, the burden of this particular book is to examine in as much detail as possible what *kind* of people the Elijah People are, to discuss their essential qualities, values and characteristics, their motivation and inner life, and what qualifies them to be the Elijah People in the first place. I trust that the reader will bear with me concerning this emphasis; in pursuing this path I believe I am following the example of the apostle Peter:

> *The day of the Lord will come like a thief. The heavens will disappear with a roar; the elements*

will be destroyed by fire, and the earth and everything in it will be laid bare. Since everything will be destroyed in this way, <u>what kind of people ought you to be?</u> You ought to live holy and godly lives as you look forward to the day of God and speed its coming. (2Peter 3:10-12)

ONE

Biblical Restoration

You will be called Repairer of Broken Walls,
Restorer of Streets with Dwellings. (Isaiah 58:12)

We usually think of the word *restoration* in terms of repairing something in order to return it to its original condition or former glory: perhaps a piece of antique furniture or an old building. Time may have taken its toll and the piece of furniture has suffered a considerable amount of wear and tear. Or the building has been neglected and become dilapidated and stands in need of renovation, repair, and probably a great amount of finance spent on it. In order to restore something in this way, we have to know what it looked like in its original condition and how it will look when it is restored to that condition. While biblical restoration certainly involves in part some kind of return to an original condition, that is only one aspect of it. Biblical restoration is a restoration to God's original and ultimate intention, not merely an original condition. This is what I will explain in this chapter. Let's begin with the passage in Acts mentioned in the previous chapter. Peter said:

"Therefore repent and turn again, so that your sins may be wiped away, in order that times of refreshing may come from the presence of the

> Lord; and that He may send Jesus, the Christ
> appointed for you, whom heaven must receive
> until the times of restoration of all things about
> which God spoke by the mouth of his holy
> prophets from ancient time." (Acts 3:19-21)

Directly before his statement concerning the restoration of all things, Peter declared that our personal repentance and faith in the Lord Jesus Christ has three important consequences:

First, *our sins may be wiped away* (verse 19). Hallelujah! When we put our faith in Jesus to save us from our sins and we confess him as our Lord we are born again by the Holy Spirit into the kingdom of God. All our sins are forgiven and we become new creations in Christ (2Corinthians 5:17). We then bury that old life, that person who has died, in the waters of baptism. The Lord Jesus Christ himself now lives in us in all his righteousness and fullness through the Person of God the Holy Spirit:

> I have been crucified with Christ, and I no longer
> live, but Christ lives in me. The life I live in the
> body I live by faith in the Son of God, who loved
> me and gave himself for me. (Galatians 2:20)

As wonderful as that is, sadly too many Christians stop here. They think that the purpose of their life is merely to be saved from their sins and one day go to heaven. However, while it is a miracle to have one's sins forgiven and to have a guaranteed place in heaven, there is so much more to Christianity than that. God has a plan! He did not create us merely to save us from our sin: he created us in order to fill the earth with a people in his image, a people who are like him:

> God said, "Let us make man in our image, in our likeness, and let them rule over the fish of the sea and the birds of the air, over the livestock, over all the earth, and over all the creatures that move along the ground." So God created man in his own image, in the image of God he created him; male and female he created them. God blessed them and said to them, "Be fruitful and increase in number; fill the earth and subdue it. Rule over the fish of the sea and the birds of the air and over every living creature that moves on the ground." (Genesis 1:26-28)

We were saved from sin so that we could play our unique part in fulfilling God's original purpose and ultimate intention for humanity that has never changed: to fill the whole world with a people like his Son. E.W. Kenyon said, "Christianity is not a religion, it is a family: a Father and his children."

Second, *that times of refreshing may come from the presence of the Lord* (verse 20). The phrase 'times of refreshing' literally means 'recovering of breath'. If you study Church history you will notice that within a relatively short time after the close of the first century AD, increasing dimensions of the Church became institutional and bound by empty traditions, rather than living in the power of the Holy Spirit and by the Word of God. By and large the Church was no longer the vibrant community of simple faith where Jesus was Lord; it was more like a political structure wielding the power of men instead of exercising the loving and holy authority of God. Biblical practices and patterns were replaced, to a large extent, by human traditions and patterns. When Christianity became the official religion of the Roman Empire in the fourth century, this process became even more pronounced as a religious system replaced the Church the New Testament describes.

Even the New Testament Church, however, was sometimes prone to this tendency to replace the teaching of the apostles and the centrality of the Spirit of Jesus with their own preferences, religious practices and even heresies. The greatest danger to the early Church was the threat from false teachers who advocated erroneous views and beliefs which destroyed the faith of many believers. The apostles constantly warned the Church against such people. The Church in Jerusalem, for example, had a faction that insisted on all male believers being circumcised (see Acts 15). This heresy caused considerable trouble to the Church in Antioch and for a time had the potential to divide the entire, wider Church across Jewish and Gentile lines. In Corinth the believers allowed immorality and double standards in the Church. The Churches in Galatia were legalistic and religious; the Church in Ephesus was accused by God of having left its first love of Jesus; the Church in Laodicea became lukewarm towards the Lord and was marked out as being smug and self-satisfied. We must never become nostalgic when we read the New Testament. Restoration is not about returning to an imagined or supposedly ideal New Testament Church: it is all to do with moving on to God's original and ultimate intention for the Church.

Nevertheless, ever since Pentecost there have been times of refreshing from the presence of the Lord. These are seasons in history when God moves powerfully by the Holy Spirit, and the form and shape of the Church subsequently changes to become more of what it should be in his original intention. In each of these times of refreshing the Holy Spirit restores to the Church what was previously eroded and replaced with man-made structures: things like believer's baptism; the baptism in the Holy Spirit; biblical patterns of ministry instead of the clergy/laity divide; personal faith in Jesus instead of gaining God's approval through our own righteous acts; the supremacy of the Word of God over human tradition; an increase in miracle power and emphasis on evangelism. Events such as the Reformation in the sixteenth century, the outpouring of the Holy Spirit at the beginning of the twentieth century in what has become known as the Pentecostal Revival, and the so-called Charismatic Movement of the 1960s and '70s are just a few examples. After each of these times of refreshing something was restored to the Church. God has never been interested in creating new denominations or renewing existing ones: he is restoring his Church to his original intention for it. Denominations remain after the Spirit of God has moved on in his restoration purpose and Christians fail to keep moving forward with him. We should also note that even before the momentous events of the Reformation, in fact right from the earliest times when the Church began to decline into formal, institutional religion, there were always radical groups of believers who strove to restore the Church to authentic Christianity. Some of them are well known, such as the Lollards and Waldensians; others are only known by the historic records, which graphically record their suffering and even destruction at the hands of the institutionalised Church.

Unfortunately the problem has often been that those who experience the previous time of refreshing in God's restoration purpose get stuck in it, own it for themselves, label it, and do not recognise and embrace the next time of refreshing. This is because they do not see that God's restoration plan is bigger than their own doctrinal bias or revelation. In fact, they sometimes ignore or even persecute those who spearhead the next move. Martin Luther (1483-1546), for example, a courageous man and one of the great Reformers who did much to restore the truth of justification by faith to the Church, persecuted those he and the other Reformers disparagingly called Anabaptists (the re-baptisers). The Anabaptists saw beyond justification by faith, beyond what Luther taught, and practised biblical believer's baptism. They correctly taught that infant baptism has no scriptural basis; in doing so they directly contradicted and opposed Luther. Eventually, they were accused by the Reformers of being too radical, because, in addition to their correct views on water baptism, they also rightly advocated the separation of Church and state (a massive issue in those days); they emphasised practical righteousness and opposed a mixed Church of both believers and non-believers (which Luther was prepared to accept). They also used the gifts of the Holy Spirit. Luther and his fellow Reformers Zwingli and Calvin disagreed so much with them that they approved the persecution and, on occasion, even the execution of the Anabaptists. One of the early Anabaptist leaders, Felix Manz, was bound with ropes and drowned by followers of the Reformers in the river Limmat in Zurich. These radical Restorers suffered terribly at the hands of the Reformers.

I was raised a Baptist; we derided the Pentecostals because they spoke in tongues. I was taught that speaking in tongues came from the devil. Many evangelical Christians in the 1960s and '70s taught that those who began to restore the truth that apostles exist today, such as the leaders of the Apostolic Church and men like Bryn Jones and Arthur Wallis, were heretics. This tendency to attack or dismiss what actually is a major move of God is often defended by appeals to doctrinal purity, Church history or denominational tradition. While it is true we must always be wise and careful in assessing new movements (Christians can be amazingly gullible at times), we should also heed the warning that Gamaliel gave the Sanhedrin when they arrested the early apostles:

"If this plan or this undertaking is of man, it will fail; but if it is of God, you will not be able to overthrow them. You might even be found opposing God!" (Acts 5:38-39)

Third, that God *may send the Christ* (verse 20). Of course, this is a direct reference to the Second Coming of Jesus in the Final Judgement on the Great and Glorious Day (Acts 2:20). Jesus will return to this world only when all the times of refreshing – the times of recovery – are complete, and all things spoken by the prophets are restored. Therefore, we must understand that our personal salvation in Christ has a much greater purpose than obtaining a ticket to heaven when we die, or even being actively involved in what God is doing today without understanding that God is doing something eternal and lasting, beyond our time. Our salvation is part of God's wonderful restoration purpose. And as we shall discover, the Church has a unique role to play in that restoration purpose.

Let's now examine more closely the meaning of biblical restoration. We will discover that it has two important aspects.

1. Recovering what has been lost

The Greek word for restoration used in Acts 3:21 is *apokatastasis*. It was a term commonly used in everyday language outside the New Testament. It basically meant to return something to its original order, and was used to describe various things like repairing a road, returning hostages and restoring property to its rightful order. It was also used to describe the re-emergence of the sun or moon after an eclipse; and the betterment of one's life by improving one's circumstances or state of affairs. This word also often occurs in various forms in the New Testament and in the Septuagint (the Greek translation of the Old Testament), where it refers to the recovery of a former condition, both physical and circumstantial:

Jesus said to the man, "Stretch out your hand." So he stretched it out and it was completely restored, just as sound as the other. (Matthew 12:13)

Once more Jesus put his hands on the man's eyes. Then his eyes were opened, his sight was restored, and he saw everything clearly. (Mark 8:25)

I particularly urge you to pray so that I may be restored to you soon. (Hebrews 13:19)

"Within three days Pharaoh will lift up your head and restore you to your position, and you will put Pharaoh's cup in his hand, just as you used to do when you were his cupbearer"... He restored the chief cupbearer to his position, so that he once again put the cup into Pharaoh's hand. (Genesis 40:13,21)

Taking this same word to refer to Jesus' return, we see that the first aspect of restoration that must take place before his coming is to set things back into their original order and condition: to recover what has been lost. For example, believer's baptism is now universally practised and accepted as integral to Christian foundations, as it was in the New Testament; it is no longer something that the Church has to contend for. It has largely been restored across the Church worldwide. Those Christians who still reject the need for believer's baptism not only deny the clear teaching of Scripture: happily, they are also in a diminishing minority.

2. Compensation: more than at first

The second aspect of restoration is the one that distinguishes biblical restoration from our normal concept of the term. In the Bible we find a detailed principle of compensatory restitution or restoration: adding something extra to what is recovered that was not there in the first place. The Law of Moses, for example, often demonstrated this principle of compensation:

Yahweh said to Moses: "When anyone is unfaithful to Yahweh by sinning unintentionally in regard to any of Yahweh's holy things, they are to bring to Yahweh as a penalty a ram from the flock, one without defect and of the proper value in silver, according to the sanctuary shekel. It is a guilt offering. <u>They must make restitution for what they have failed to do in regard to the holy things, pay an additional penalty of a fifth of its value and give it all to the priest.</u> The priest will make atonement for them with the ram as a guilt offering, and they will be forgiven." (Leviticus 5:14-16)

Yahweh said to Moses, "Say to the Israelites: 'Any man or woman who wrongs another in any way and so is unfaithful to Yahweh is guilty and must confess the sin they have committed. <u>They must make full restitution for the wrong they have done, add a fifth of the value to it and give it all to the person they have wronged.</u>"' (Numbers 5:5-7)

In the case of stolen items double the original value had to be returned (see Exodus 22:4,7,9). Restoration in the Old Testament involved paying back the full value of what was lost (recovery) plus adding compensation of anything between twenty percent and one hundred percent. This principle of compensation, what I call the *overplus*, is also found in the life of Job. Most of us know his story: how he lost everything through no fault of his own. However, we must not forget the end of Job's story:

Yahweh restored the fortunes of Job... And Yahweh gave Job twice as much as he had before...

And Yahweh blessed the latter days of Job more than his beginning. (Job 42:10, 12)

This is true restoration: even though Job lost all he had, not only did he recover it, God also added in compensation to him far more than he had lost. If we compare the beginning and end of the story we find that Job originally had seven sons and three daughters. Sadly they all died. Not only did God give him seven more sons and three more daughters, it is said of these three ladies that: *In all the land there were no women as beautiful as Job's daughters. And their father gave them an inheritance among their brothers* (Job 42:15). Job also lived to see his sons' sons and grandchildren to the fourth generation. At the beginning of his story, Job owned seven thousand sheep, three thousand camels, five hundred oxen and five hundred female donkeys (Job 1:2-3). When God restored the fortunes of Job he had double what he had lost (Job 42:12).

In the New Testament we find the example of compensatory restoration in Zacchaeus. He was a Jewish tax collector who collaborated with the Roman occupiers and extorted vast amounts of money from his fellow citizens. He grew extremely rich from his ill-gotten gains. Then he met Jesus. That encounter transformed Zacchaeus to the extent that he recompensed all those he had defrauded four times what he had stolen from them, and gave half his remaining wealth to the poor (Luke 19:8-10).

Then of course is the matter of our salvation. First of all, when we repent and put our faith in Jesus, he forgives all our sins and completely removes them from us (Psalm 103:12). We are no longer sinners, which is wonderful.

However, God does not stop there: we do not live as forgiven sinners. Because God is a Restorer, he also gives us something we never had in the first place – the righteousness of Christ:

> He made him to be sin who knew no sin, so that in him we might become the righteousness of God. (2Corinthians 5:21)

This is the compensation element of our salvation: as new creations in Christ, we have far more than Adam originally possessed and lost. We are not saved to be restored to the same original condition that Adam experienced: we have much more. In Christ we have God the Holy Spirit indwelling us with the righteous nature of Jesus. God's mercy and grace are the two sides of our personal restoration. They are the restoring love of God in action:

> Because of his great love for us, God, who is rich in mercy, made us alive with Christ even when we were dead in transgressions – it is by grace you have been saved. (Ephesians 2:4-5)

> In him [Jesus] we have redemption through his blood, the forgiveness of sins, in accordance with the riches of God's grace that he lavished on us with all wisdom and understanding. (Ephesians 1:7-8)

In expressing to us his loving mercy, God does not give us what we deserve: spiritual death, punishment for our sins, and eternal separation from God in hell.

Because God is rich in mercy, when we come to him and ask him for mercy, he gladly gives it, because he loves us so much. That is the wonder of what Jesus has done in dying for us and rising from the dead. Daniel understood the nature and power of God's mercy. When he prayed and pleaded with God to begin the work of restoring God's people and to return them to their land, he appealed to the mercy of God:

We do not make requests of you because we are righteous, but because of your great mercy. O Lord, listen! O Lord, forgive! O Lord, hear and act! (Daniel 9:18-19)

God, however, not only shows us mercy, he also lavishes his grace on us. In his mercy he does not give us what we deserve; but he goes further and also gives us what we do not deserve. That is how grace works. We did not deserve forgiveness of our sins and the gift of righteous sonship: but that is what God gave us. We have something extra, an overplus: we are the righteousness of God in Christ! This is the compensation element of our salvation. This process of compensation continues the rest of our lives as we mature in our relationship with God as his sons. We will have more to say about this in a subsequent chapter.

In a real sense, our restoration even continues even after we die. We can say that even Jesus had a restoration: he died and his body was laid in a tomb. But three days later he rose again to a resurrection life. He did not merely come back to life: he was resurrected and will never die again. Jesus received a resurrection body when he rose from the dead; and he has that body now. Likewise, for all those Christians who die before Jesus returns, they too will receive a resurrection body when he comes. Those who are alive at his return will not see death but immediately be changed and receive their resurrection body (see 1Corinthians 15:12-58; 1Thessalonians 4:13-18). Our resurrection bodies will not age or decay; they will never get sick or suffer pain and death. That is true restoration.

Keep moving forwards

These biblical examples demonstrate that restoration is not only recovering what has been lost but also includes the vital element of compensation: adding what was not there in the first place. Restoration, therefore, does not mean God intends us merely to go backwards in an attempt to return the Church to some nostalgic, ideal, original condition of purity that is supposed to have existed in the early Church. Restoration certainly does include the recovery of all that was good in the New Testament Church: repentance, faith, water baptism, baptism in the Holy Spirit, Ephesians 4 ministries, family life, the gifts and power of the Spirit, personal righteousness, covenant oneness and radical discipleship, to name a few. We must commend the early Church in this regard. They also were involved in God's restoration purpose and within a generation had spread the Gospel of the Kingdom throughout much of the known world. They impacted societies and even posed a threat to the might of the Roman Empire, who at certain times persecuted them intensely. It was, as the author and New Testament translator J.B. Phillips commented, the young Church in action. A.W. Tozer made this observation about the early Church:

The early Church was not an organisation, nor a movement, but a walking incarnation of spiritual energy. The Church began in power, moved in power and moved just as long as she had power. When she no longer had power she dug in for safety and sought to conserve her gains.

Nevertheless, as I have already pointed out, the Church of the New Testament was not the perfect model some mistake it for. Therefore, we must not accept God's intention for the Church only on what we see in the pages of the Acts of the Apostles, no matter how exciting and challenging they might be. Neither is restoration an attempt to return to the innocence and purity of the Garden of Eden. Let me emphasise again: we are not restored to the original condition of Adam and Eve before they sinned. Restoration is all about looking and moving forward to what has not yet been. Abraham looked forward to a city (Hebrews 11:10); the book of Revelation speaks of the restored Bride of Christ in terms of a Garden City, not the Garden of Eden restored (Revelation 21 and 22). Restoration is advancement to the fullness of God's pre-Fall original intention for the earth and for a humanity created in his image which has yet to be fully realised in and through the Church. In the words of Bryn Jones:

Restoration is the action of God to accomplish his purpose of bringing all things back into total harmony with himself, and his moving everything in heaven and earth forward to the fullness of his original intention for them.

Therefore, restoration must not be viewed as a work of God that affects only the Church; restoration is a purpose that embraces all the prophets spoke of concerning things in heaven as well as earth: it is the restoration of all things. This purpose is encapsulated in Ephesians 1:9-10:

And he made known to us the mystery of his will according to his good pleasure, which he purposed in Christ, to be put into effect when the times will have reached their fulfilment - to bring all things in heaven and earth under one head, even Christ.

The sole reason for the Church's existence lies within this wonderful, miraculous reality; the Church as the agent of the kingdom of God on earth is the chosen means by which God achieves his purpose in Christ in this age: to bring all things under the headship of Jesus. This is the unique purpose of the Church:

His intent was that now, through the Church, the manifold wisdom of God should be made known to the rulers and authorities in the heavenly realms, according to his eternal purpose which he accomplished in Christ Jesus our Lord. (Ephesians 3:10-11)

The Lord Jesus Christ is the means and the object of the restoration purpose of God: he is the last Adam and the second man (1Corinthians 15:45-49); he is the Seed of the woman (Genesis 3:15) and the Seed of Abraham (Galatians 3:16), who has redeemed for himself a people who will fulfil the original mandate of being recreated in true righteousness and holiness, and thus fill the earth with the life of God. Jesus is the Head of the Body and the Bridegroom of the Bride. Jesus is the centre and circumference of God's restoration purpose. The means by which Jesus will restore all things to the original intention of God is through the people who have believed on his name. The New Testament calls these people Christians, believers, brothers and sisters, the sons of God, the Church of God, the Body of Christ, the Bride of Christ, and the household of God. This is who the Elijah People are.

God has placed us on earth as his redeemed Elijah People to implement and establish something that the world has not yet seen in his Church. We are here to see all things restored to God's original and ultimate intention, and so hasten the coming of the Lord Jesus.

TWO

Three Elijahs

*Elijah is coming and will restore
all things. (Matthew 17:11)*

We have established that Jesus must remain in heaven
until the restoration of all things 'spoken by the
prophets' (Acts 3:21). One of the major prophecies
spoken by the prophets about the coming again of the
Lord Jesus in Final Judgement is found in Malachi, the
last book of the Old Testament. It concerns one of the
greatest Old Testament prophets, Elijah:

*See, I will send you the prophet Elijah before that
great and dreadful day of Yahweh comes. He will
turn the hearts of the fathers to their children, and
the hearts of the children to their fathers; or else
I will come and strike the land with a curse.
(Malachi 4:5-6)*

The 'great and dreadful day' mentioned here is a
direct reference to the Second Coming of Jesus Christ. In
the Bible you will often come across the phrase 'the day
of the Lord' (Joel 2:31; 1Thessalonians 5:2; 2Peter 3:10).
Sometimes, as in these cases, it is a reference to the
climax of earth's history when God will come in Final

Judgement: the actual day when Jesus will return in glory to usher in the new age.

At Pentecost, as Peter preached to the crowd and explained what they were witnessing as they stared in jaw-dropping amazement at one hundred and twenty people filled with the Holy Spirit, he quoted the Old Testament prophet Joel, who hundreds of years earlier had prophesied about the great and glorious day of the Lord:

The sun will be turned to darkness and the moon to blood before the coming of the great and glorious day of the Lord. And everyone who calls on the name of the Lord will be saved. (Acts 2:20-21, quoting Joel 2:31-32)

The phrase 'the sun will be turned to darkness and the moon to blood' is symbolic language describing the rise and fall of nations and empires. The 'great and glorious day' of Joel is the same as the 'great and dreadful day' of Malachi: the Second Coming of Jesus. Joel describes what will happen to the world; Malachi describes the kind of Church that will hasten the Lord's return. Remember, we are primarily concerned in this study with the quality of the Church that Jesus will return for. Malachi gives us an idea of what kind of people the Church will increasingly become as the Elijah People before the Second Coming of Jesus.

Malachi was the last of the Old Testament prophets; he prophesied regarding the coming of the Lord Jesus in Final Judgement in approximately 440 BC, asserting that before this history-defining event, Elijah will also come. However, by the time of Malachi, the prophet Elijah had already been gone for over four hundred years. Elijah lived around 900-850 BC and was taken up to heaven in a whirlwind without dying (2Kings 2:11). Furthermore, when Malachi prophesied about Jesus' Second Coming and Elijah's role in it, Jesus had not yet come for the first time to be born in Bethlehem; that was still four hundred and forty years in the future.

What does Malachi's prophecy mean?

Luke's gospel opens with a direct reference to Elijah. The angel Gabriel visited Zechariah the priest and told him all about the son he and his wife Elizabeth would have - John the Baptist:

> *"He will be great before the Lord. And he must not drink wine or strong drink, and he will be filled with the Holy Spirit, even from his mother's womb. And he will turn many of the children of Israel to the Lord their God, and he will go before him <u>in the spirit and power of Elijah</u>, to turn the hearts of the fathers to the children, and the disobedient to the wisdom of the righteous, to make ready for the Lord a people prepared." (Luke 1:15-17)*

Gabriel informed Zechariah that his son, John the Baptist, would go before the Lord in the spirit and power of Elijah. This phrase 'go before him in the spirit and power of Elijah' means he would act as a forerunner, as one who would prepare the way for the Lord. This is what John the Baptist did; look how he described himself:

> *John replied in the words of Isaiah the prophet, "I am the voice of one calling in the wilderness, 'Make straight the way for the Lord.'" (John 1:23)*

Was John the Baptist the 'Elijah' that Malachi prophesied about? In part, yes he was; but, as we shall see, he was not the ultimate fulfilment of the prophecy. Just over thirty years after Gabriel's declaration, Jesus himself also spoke of Elijah and John the Baptist. By this time both Jesus and John the Baptist were prominent in their public ministries, and John was in prison, awaiting execution. Jesus took the opportunity to address the crowds concerning him, since John had intrigued them, provoked them, challenged them and affected many of them deeply. At the same time Jesus also spoke prophetically of all those who would enter the kingdom of God through faith in him and their comparison to John the Baptist. Jesus identified John the Baptist with Elijah:

> *"I tell you the truth: Among those born of women there has not risen anyone greater than John the Baptist; yet he who is least in the kingdom of heaven is greater than he. From the days of John the Baptist until now, the kingdom of heaven has been forcefully advancing, and forceful men lay hold of it. For all the Prophets and the Law prophesied until John. And if you are willing to accept it, he is the Elijah who was to come."* (Matthew 11:11-14)

John the Baptist was not Elijah. The Jews of Jesus' time knew that Elijah had not died but had been taken up to heaven while still alive (2Kings 2:11). They believed from Malachi 4:5 that he would come back to earth to pronounce what they understood as the end times, in preparation for the coming of the Lord. Of course, their understanding of this event did not equate to what Christians believe: that the coming of the Lord is all to do with Jesus Christ. They also lived with a heightened sense of Messianic expectation because of the Roman occupation of their land. The nation was anticipating a political and military deliverer like King David – a Messiah figure – to rise up, drive out the Romans in a revolution, and restore Israel to its glorious past as it had been when David ruled, a thousand years previously. John the Baptist, however, constantly and emphatically denied that he was Elijah: *They asked him, "Then who are you? Are you Elijah?" He said, "I am not"* (John 1:21). They asked John this question because he looked like Elijah, he dressed like Elijah, he behaved like Elijah, and so reminded the people of Elijah:

> *The king asked them, "What kind of man was it who came to meet you and told you this?" They replied, "He was a man with a garment of hair and with a leather belt around his waist." The king said, "That was Elijah the Tishbite." (2Kings 1:7-8).*

> *John's clothes were made of camel's hair, and he had a leather belt around his waist. His food was locusts and wild honey. (Matthew 3:4)*

John the Baptist dressed and acted this way quite deliberately. He made it abundantly clear that he was not Elijah come back to earth or reincarnated. His purpose in behaving in this manner was to demonstrate that he was a forerunner, preparing the way for the one who would come after him. He thus purposely identified himself with Elijah. However, he knew that he was not the ultimate Elijah that Malachi had spoken about. John deliberately provoked those who came to see him, vividly demonstrating to them the fact that through him the ministry of Elijah was active among them. Coming in the 'spirit and power' of Elijah, he had an Elijah-type of ministry. He declared to his hearers, as Elijah had done in his lifetime, that God was in their midst: in encountering John they encountered God himself; in meeting him they met God himself; when he spoke, God spoke. He reminded them that the challenges that Elijah made to his generation were still relevant; that God's purpose and demands on his people were still the same as they had been in Elijah's time. He provoked and challenged his generation to prepare themselves for the One coming after him – Jesus.

Elijah and the Transfiguration

Soon after John the Baptist's death at the hands of Herod, Jesus took Peter, James and John with him up a high mountain:

There he was transfigured before them. His face shone like the sun, and his clothes became as white as the light. Just then there appeared before them Moses and Elijah, talking with Jesus. (Matthew 17:2-3)

Here were two of the major characters of the Old Testament: Moses, the original giver of the law of God, and the prophet Elijah, whose prophetic ministry and message to the people of his time had been an attempt to restore them to the righteous ways of the law. These giants of the Old Testament were deep in conversation with Jesus concerning his imminent suffering and death. Naturally, as the three disciples came down the mountain with Jesus after such an incredible experience, they had questions:

Jesus' disciples asked him, "Why do the scribes say that Elijah must come first?" He replied, "Elijah is coming and will restore all things; but I say to you that Elijah already came, and they did not recognise him, but did to him whatever they wished. So also the Son of Man is going to suffer at their hands." Then the disciples understood that he had spoken to them about John the Baptist. (Matthew 17:10-13)

Like other Jews of the time, Peter, James and John believed from Malachi 4:5 that Elijah would come before the Messiah's arrival. If Jesus was the Messiah, as they believed him to be, why hadn't Elijah appeared? Jesus' reply to the question came at two levels. He answered them *at* their level of revelation and understanding, and *beyond* their level of revelation and understanding. He spoke into their immediate situation, explaining John the Baptist's relationship to Elijah and therefore to him as Messiah. Then he spoke about the wider, eternal restoration purpose of God; he spoke into our time, the age of the Church as the agent of the kingdom of God. Firstly, Jesus said that Elijah *had* come before him, but they did not recognise him as such, despite John's obvious similarity to Elijah. Elijah had 'come' in the person of John the Baptist. Secondly, and of greater significance, Jesus then spoke of an Elijah who 'is coming and will restore all things'. By this time Herod had beheaded John the Baptist and all things were not yet restored. Remember how we defined restoration in the previous chapter: John the Baptist did not restore all things to God's original intention. He had not brought about the necessary recovery and compensation of the restoration of all things that Peter would later refer to in Acts 3:21. Therefore, there must be another Elijah besides Elijah himself and John the Baptist: there is an Elijah who will restore all things.

Three 'Elijahs'

As has now become evident, the Bible presents us with three 'Elijahs':

1. Elijah himself;
2. John the Baptist (who came in the spirit and power of Elijah);
3. The Elijah who is coming and will restore all things.

We have established that before Jesus comes again God will send the prophet Elijah (Malachi 4:5-6). We have the original Elijah and the 'second' Elijah – John the Baptist – who came in the spirit and power of Elijah, with an Elijah 'type' of ministry. He would be like Elijah and act like Elijah and have the same effect as Elijah. Both of them have gone from the earth and the restoration of all things is still incomplete. Therefore, we are left with one more 'Elijah': the 'Elijah who is coming and will restore all things'. In John the Baptist, who prepared the way for Jesus' first coming, there was a partial fulfilment. However, it is only in the 'Elijah who is coming', who will prepare the way for Jesus' Second Coming, that the Malachi prophecy will be finally and completely fulfilled.

That John was not in the fullest sense the Elijah of Malachi 4 is clear: the Elijah who is to come will do so prior to the final Day of the Lord – the Second Coming of Jesus. The Elijah who is to come will restore **all** things, which John did not accomplish. Most importantly, remember that the restoration of all things was still not yet complete by the time Peter spoke in Acts 3:21, much later on than this incident. Peter stated that the restoration of all things still lay in the future.

Who is the third Elijah?

Since John the Baptist was not a reincarnation of the Old Testament character, there is no reason for us to suppose that the third Elijah will be. The Bible does not teach reincarnation. The Elijah who is coming is not a single individual, nor a super saint. While it is true that the Bible demonstrates Elijah's solitariness, that is only because it uses this facet of the prophet's life to display that he lived in stark contrast to his world and society. We also see this in John the Baptist's life and ministry, but we also discover that he had a company of disciples, some of whom he directed to become disciples of Jesus, while others remained with him until his death (Matthew 14:12; John 1:35-37).

We discover in the New Testament that God works through, and is represented by, a people: his Kingdom community, the Church. The whole emphasis in the New Testament is on a people, the Body of Christ; brothers and sisters; the family of God; the sons of God; the household of God. These are all corporate images. In the New Testament Church there is no super omni-compotent individual in whom God invests all his life and purpose. The New Testament constantly affirms the corporate over the independent, isolated and individualistic. If we are not careful we can misinterpret Paul's letters through forgetting that by and large they were written to communities. There is only one individual Person that God has invested his purpose in: the Lord Jesus Christ, who expresses his life on earth through a people. Jesus is the Head of his Body, the Church, the Elijah People.

What about Revelation 11?

This concept of a corporate Elijah is even seen in Revelation 11:3-12 in the form of the two witnesses, widely acknowledged as representing Moses and Elijah. They are not specifically called Moses or Elijah in the passage, but they demonstrate their characteristics and act like them. Concerning those characteristics and actions of the Elijah figure, note that even these are corporate:

- They have power to shut up the sky (Revelation 11:6);
- Their presence is a challenge and provocation to those who live on earth (Revelation 11:10);
- They go up to heaven in a cloud (Revelation 11:12).

It is vitally important that we avoid weird interpretations of the Bible in general and of Revelation in particular. This last book of the Bible is a revealing of Jesus (Revelation 1:1), written to believers, and it was not intended to confuse or confound them. The book of Revelation made sense to its readers. Sadly many modern interpretations and commentaries ignore this simple fact. What does this passage in Revelation 11 mean? Tony Ling gives an excellent explanation:

ROGER AUBREY

*[This passage] represents to us the whole
Church age, the whole age in which the Church is
ministering in the name of Jesus, in which we are
supposed to demonstrate our power and authority,
and in which we are supposed to move in signs and
wonders – to reproduce, if you like, the ministry of
Elijah in our world.*

The least is greater

*Among those born of women there has not risen
anyone greater than John the Baptist; yet he who
is least in the kingdom of heaven is greater than he.
(Matthew 11:11)*

Here Jesus points directly to the identity and nature
of the third Elijah; it is those who are in the kingdom
of God: the Kingdom community, the Church.
Undoubtedly, John the Baptist was a major figure in
God's eternal purpose. He prepared the way for Jesus to
be revealed as the Lamb of God, the Saviour of the World,
and the Baptiser in the Holy Spirit (John 1:29; Matthew
3:11). Jesus freely acknowledged that his cousin and
friend was a great man, one of the greatest who ever lived
up to that time. John was the last of the Old Covenant
prophets, even though he is featured in the New
Testament.

The remarkable truth is that anybody who has been
born again, anybody who has received Jesus as Lord and
Saviour and entered the kingdom of God is greater than
John the Baptist. That is astounding. As Jesus said: even
those who *think* they are least in the Kingdom are in fact
greater than John. We have been born again into the
restoration purpose of God! Anybody in the kingdom of

God is part of the Elijah People. As I will deal with later: many Christians have to stop thinking wrongly about themselves and start seeing themselves as God sees them. Their lives will be transformed, and their effectiveness in the cause of Christ will increase.

Let me say it again: all of us who are in the kingdom of God are greater than John the Baptist: we have a greater role to play than John; we make a greater impact on the world's history than he did. How can that be? Because Jesus said so. We as the Elijah People, as the restorers of all things, are the forerunners who prepare the way for the Lord Jesus Christ to return in glory. There is no greater calling. Since Jesus is your Lord, you have a unique role to play as part of the Elijah People. That is why you are greater than John the Baptist: God has called you to be part of his Church, his Elijah People, involved in his restoration purpose. It is time for the Church as the Elijah People to grow up and be the mature manifestation of God in the world that restores all things spoken by the prophets and hastens the return of the Lord Jesus.

THREE

The Back Story

Ahab son of Omri did more evil in the eyes of Yahweh than any of those before him. (1Kings 16:30)

In preparation for the following chapters it would be good for us to have some background information on the person of Elijah. It will be helpful for us to understand who he was and the kind of society that he lived in. We must always remember that the Bible characters were real people living in a real world. They faced real pressures, real situations, real opposition, real power. They were just like us. When we put the men and women of the Bible into their historical and cultural context, we increasingly discover that they faced many of the issues we face today. We thus learn from their example, and are encouraged in our faith. The more we explore the lives of the biblical characters we find that their lives are extremely relevant to ours.

A house divided

After the death of King Solomon in 930 BC, the kingdom of Israel divided in two (see 1Kings 12:1-24). Solomon was succeeded by his son Rehoboam, who did something very foolish. He listened to unwise counsel concerning how he should treat the ten northern tribes of the nation, and he consequently imposed harsh conditions on them. As a result the northern part of the nation refused Rehoboam's kingship and broke away to form a separate kingdom. Thereafter the books of First and Second Kings refer to the northern kingdom of the ten tribes, called Israel, with its capital in Samaria, and the southern kingdom of two tribes – Judah and Benjamin – called Judah, with its capital in Jerusalem. The southern kings of Judah were all descendants of Solomon and his father, King David. They were a mixture of good kings (such as Josiah and Hezekiah) and evil kings (like Ahaz and Manasseh).

Jeroboam was the first king of the new northern kingdom of Israel after its division from Judah. He was a long-standing adversary of Solomon and had led the rebellion against Rehoboam. Not surprisingly, he claimed the throne of Israel for himself. Jeroboam subtly instituted the false religion of Baalism into the nation through the idolatrous worship of golden calves, to prevent the people from going down to Jerusalem, the capital of Judah, to worship Yahweh in the temple Solomon had built many years previously. His motives in this were political as well as religious. He did not want the new nation of Israel to be influenced by the southern kingdom of Judah in any way, because it might weaken his position. Jeroboam thus began a process that turned the northern kingdom of Israel increasingly away from Yahweh.

Jeroboam's successors actively continued what he had started. Every subsequent king of the northern kingdom of Israel was as bad as, or worse than, his predecessor. In 874 BC, Ahab succeeded his father Omri as king of Israel. This is how the Bible introduces him:

Ahab son of Omri did more evil in the eyes of Yahweh than any of those before him. (1 Kings 16:30)

With Ahab, the idolatry of Israel reached its all time high, with systematic attempts to eradicate completely the worship of Yahweh. Ahab was a morally weak man, yet at the same time he was a master schemer, petulant, sly, devious and highly politically motivated. He married Jezebel, the daughter of Ethbaal, who was king of the Sidonians and a priest of the Canaanite god Baal-Melqart. Jezebel was also an active worshipper of this false god. She wielded a great deal of influence and power over Ahab, who permitted Jezebel to introduce into God's covenant people the particular worship of Baal-Melqart. The previous generations of Israelites had encountered Baalism before, but now the nation's rulers and leaders, both political and spiritual, not only sanctioned that same idolatry, but also actively promoted it under Ahab and Jezebel. In doing so, they turned the hearts of the people further and further away from Yahweh. Jezebel did not want the worship of Baal-Melqart to co-exist with that of Yahweh, so she instituted a campaign of terror against the prophets of Yahweh in an attempt to eliminate them completely. Baal-Melqart was believed to be the god of the rain and clouds; he supposedly gave the land its fertility. Thus he was believed to be the god of the crops that the land produced. Under Ahab, Baal-Melqart worship became the official religion of Israel and the worship of Yahweh, to all intents and purposes, was forbidden. This was compounded even more when Jezebel began murdering Yahweh's prophets.

The promotion of idolatry in Israel was accompanied by an active unrighteousness in all areas of life. (Ungodliness and unrighteousness always go hand in hand). Society became more and more corrupt and immoral as the priests of Baal-Melqart became more prominent, and Jezebel manipulated and dominated the weak and ungodly Ahab for her own ends. Israel, the covenant people of Yahweh, became instead a people who had turned away from Yahweh and worshipped a false, non-existent god; they lived their own way, doing their own thing. It was a society that was rapidly falling apart spiritually, morally and politically. Prophets like Amos, who prophesied to Israel from around 760 to 750 BC, followed on from Elijah and his successor Elisha. However, the spiritual and moral condition of the nation continued to deteriorate; it finally crumbled completely in 722 BC when it fell to the Assyrians and the population was taken into captivity and exile. Elijah came to public prominence right in the midst of this national crisis. Here is how the Bible introduces him:

In the thirty-eighth year of Asa king of [the southern kingdom of] Judah [874BC], Ahab son of Omri became king of [the northern kingdom of] Israel, and he reigned in Samaria over Israel for twenty-two years [852BC]. Ahab son of Omri did more evil in the eyes of Yahweh than any of those before him. He not only considered it trivial to commit the sins of Jeroboam son of Nebat, but he also married Jezebel daughter of Ethbaal king of the Sidonians, and began to serve Baal [Melqart] and worship him. He set up an altar for Baal in the temple of Baal that he built in Samaria. Ahab also made an Asherah [a fertility goddess] pole and did more to provoke Yahweh, the God of Israel, to anger than did all the kings of Israel before him...

...Now Elijah the Tishbite, from Tishbe in Gilead, said to Ahab, "As Yahweh, the God of Israel, lives, whom I serve, there will be neither dew nor rain in the next few years except at my word." (1Kings 16:29 to 17:1)

The Bible does not tell us much more about Elijah than that he came from Tishbe in Gilead (the highland region east of the Jordan River, equating to the northwest of modern day Jordan). His ancestors were those who had settled on the wrong side of the Jordan, instead of going in to inherit their destiny with the other tribes under Joshua's leadership. Elijah broke that pattern of behaviour; he boldly involved himself in God's cutting edge agenda for his time and confronted Ahab and Jezebel to show them and the nation that Yahweh alone was God. He reminded them that they were Yahweh's people, and that they must repent and turn again to Yahweh to worship and serve him alone. Furthermore, he set out to demonstrate that Yahweh alone was the *living* God: that Baal-Melqart did not actually exist. He did it by entering into the midst of his world and taking on the spiritual, political, religious, and moral powers and authorities. The very first thing he did was to declare that it was not Baal-Melqart who was god of the rain and the crops: it was Yahweh, the living God. To prove it, as Yahweh's representative, the prophet of Yahweh prophesied there would be no rain until he said so. Elijah's word came true and he soon became public enemy number one. He was a wanted man. Ahab and Jezebel did all they could to track him down and destroy him.

Elijah's story is found in 1Kings 17:1 to 2Kings 2:11. It is quite a short section of the Bible and full of action. I recommend that, if possible, you read it at some point while reading the rest of this book. Next we will discover more about what kind of man Elijah was; this will help us begin to discover the characteristics and qualities of the Elijah People and how we should live accordingly.

FOUR

Who are you?

Elijah the Tishbite,
from Tishbe in Gilead... (1Kings 17:1)

"I am the voice of one calling in the desert,
'Make straight the way for the Lord.'" (John 1:23)

The first characteristic of the Elijah People we must explore is the same as the first thing we discover about Elijah himself: his identity. The Bible deliberately downplays Elijah's family life and personal details because it wants to highlight and emphasise his name. Elijah's name tells us all we need to know about his identity and, therefore, ours as the Elijah People.

The name Elijah means *Yahweh is my God.* Every time Elijah spoke his name, that is what he said: "my name is 'Yahweh is my God.'" Whenever anybody said his name, they described him as the man whose God was Yahweh. Every word Elijah spoke, everything he did and every attitude he displayed was meant to be a declaration of who he was: 'Yahweh is my God'. Elijah's name identified and consequently defined him. He behaved according to his identity; he lived up to his name.

Elijah was so identified with Yahweh in people's thinking that they almost always spoke of him in terms of his relationship and fellowship with Yahweh. For them, to encounter Elijah was to encounter Yahweh himself. They even spoke of Yahweh and Elijah in the same breath: *Elisha said, "As surely as Yahweh lives and as you live, I will not leave you"* (2Kings 2:2).

Elijah's life graphically demonstrated the fact that Yahweh was God. Anybody who met Elijah met Yahweh. Furthermore, this is how Elijah viewed himself. He was honoured and proud to be identified with Yahweh. He did not live a life in which his faith was private and personal. He was not a secret follower of Yahweh, keeping his faith to himself. Elijah's life and testimony were open to public scrutiny, and he had no problem with that. Elijah was never embarrassed to be identified with Yahweh. He was on record as being the man whose God was Yahweh, the living God. He would never compromise that fact. The first recorded words of Elijah in the Bible demonstrate this: *"As Yahweh the God of Israel lives, before whom I stand..."* (1Kings 17:1).

Elijah identified himself with Yahweh's life, Yahweh's cause, Yahweh's purpose, Yahweh's standards, Yahweh's demands and Yahweh's rule. If anybody wanted to know what Yahweh was like, all they had to do was meet Elijah. That phrase 'before whom I stand' literally describes one who stands in the presence of a king and serves him (hence the NIV's *the God whom I serve*). He consistently reminded the people that he was Yahweh's man, not only in name, but also in action. He was a constant sign to the nation that Yahweh was alive and Yahweh was God. Three and a half years after Elijah first confronted Ahab and prophesied there would be no rain until he said so, came the great confrontation with the priests of Baal-Melqart at Mount Carmel (see 1Kings

18). As he addressed Ahab and the people that day, the issue for Elijah was simple and clear:

"How long will you limp along, hesitating and wavering between two opinions? If Yahweh is God, follow him; but if Baal, then follow him." (1Kings 18:21)

Everybody knew whose side Elijah was on. Nobody ever contested his claim to be the representative of Yahweh. They accepted the fact, even if they did not like it. In the confrontation with Baal-Melqart's prophets, Elijah patiently waited all day while his opponents frantically attempted with all their might to get their non-existent god to respond. Elijah knew with absolute certainty they would not succeed. When his turn to act as the representative of Yahweh came, first of all he prayed:

"O Yahweh, God of Abraham, Isaac and Israel, let it be known today that you are God in Israel, and that I am your servant, and that I have done all these things at your word. Answer me, Yahweh, answer me, that this people may know that you, Yahweh, are God and that you are turning their hearts back again." (1Kings 18:36-37)

When the fire fell from heaven a few moments later, the people identified it as an action of Yahweh because it was performed by the man whose name was *Yahweh is my God*. They fell to the ground in repentance and worship and exclaimed: *"Yahweh, he is God; Yahweh, he is God"* (1Kings 18:39).

We should also point out that the conflict between Elijah and the prophets of Baal-Melqart was not one of irrelevant, academic theological correctness, of who should be the God or god of Israel. Elijah did not offer a choice between two equally valid contrasting philosophies or theologies. The issue was: who was alive and therefore God – Yahweh or Baal-Melqart? Elijah was not only identified with Yahweh, he was identified with Yahweh *who lives*. The practical implication of this fact was, and remains today, that the God who lives demands to be worshipped and served as the unique living God. There is only one Divine Being, one Deity who lives: Yahweh. He is the living God, the *I AM WHO I AM*. The Old Testament prophets and psalmists frequently made much of this, denouncing the imaginary gods of the other nations, especially when proponents and supporters of these false gods attempted to introduce their worship to the people of Yahweh. In this particular example, the psalmist makes a withering attack on such false, non-existent gods:

> *Their idols are silver and gold, made by the hands of men. They have mouths, but cannot speak, eyes, but they cannot see; they have ears, but cannot hear, noses, but they cannot smell; they have hands, but cannot feel, feet, but they cannot walk; nor can they utter a sound with their throats. Those who make them will be like them, and so will all who trust in them. (Psalm 115:4-8)*

John the Nazirite

We know much more about John the Baptist's personal life than Elijah's. He was Jesus' cousin; the

Gospels all mention him, and Matthew and Luke give us detailed information on his birth and family. Nevertheless this same quality that we have seen in Elijah concerning his name was also evident in John the Baptist, in particular in what he was and did. John always identified and defined himself and his ministry in relation to Jesus: *"I am not the Christ, but I have been sent before him"* (John 3:28). Furthermore, John himself constantly directed people beyond himself to the One who would come after him – Jesus. Look at some of the things he said and did in this regard:

> *"After me will come one who is more powerful than I, whose sandals I am not fit to carry."* (Matthew 3:11)

> *The next day John was there again with two of his disciples. When he saw Jesus passing by, he said, "Look, the Lamb of God!" When the two disciples heard him say this, they followed Jesus.* (John 1:35-37)

> *"He must increase, but I must decrease."* (John 3:30)

John understood that his significance in this world was not centred on himself and his own destiny. This is highlighted in the fact that John was a lifelong Nazirite, a person separated to God's purpose. The Bible tells us about such people:

> *Yahweh said to Moses, "Speak to the Israelites and say to them: 'If a man or woman wants to make a*

special vow, a vow of separation to Yahweh as a Nazirite, he must abstain from wine and other fermented drink and must not drink vinegar made from wine or from other fermented drink. He must not drink grape juice or eat grapes or raisins. As long as he is a Nazirite, he must not eat anything that comes from the grapevine, not even the seeds or skins. "'During the entire period of his vow of separation no razor may be used on his head. He must be holy until the period of his separation to Yahweh is over; he must let the hair of his head grow long. Throughout the period of his separation to Yahweh he must not go near a dead body. Even if his own father or mother or brother or sister dies, he must not make himself ceremonially unclean on account of them, because the symbol of his separation to God is on his head. Throughout the period of his separation he is consecrated to Yahweh.'" (Numbers 6:1-8)

Anybody could make a Nazirite vow of separation to God. During this period he or she would live especially consecrated and devoted to God. The Nazirite (the word means to set apart to sacred purposes) would be marked by their long hair, they could not drink alcohol, and were forbidden to go near dead bodies. These would symbolise the fact that this person was especially devoting himself or herself to God for a season. The Nazirite would, therefore, be uniquely identified with God. Some people, like Samson and Samuel, were lifelong Nazirites (Judges 13:4-7; 1Samuel 1:11). As a Nazirite, John the Baptist's physical appearance and lifestyle identified him as belonging to God and representing him through his dedication and separation to God.

The identity of the Elijah People

There is a New Testament name that identifies and defines the Elijah People: Christian. The New Testament contains several descriptions of Christians: believers, followers of the Way, brothers and sisters (Acts 4:32; Acts 6:3; Acts 9:2). However, it was the epithet Christian that quickly came to describe the Church to the world:

The disciples were called Christians first at Antioch. (Acts 11:26)

Then Agrippa said to Paul, "Do you think that in such a short time you can persuade me to be a Christian?" (Acts 26:28)

However, if you suffer as a Christian, do not be ashamed, but praise God that you bear that name. (1Peter 4:16)

The Elijah People are Christians. When the early Church encountered and interacted with the world, the world so identified these people with Jesus Christ that they called them Christians. *Christ* means Anointed One; it is the Greek form of the Hebrew word *Messiah*, which means the same. A Christian is not Christ, but is so identified with Christ that to meet a Christian is to meet Christ himself. Christians sometimes are even described as 'little Christs'.

Unfortunately, the word Christian is largely devalued today. Whenever I meet unbelievers and have opportunity to tell them about Jesus, I always say, "I am a Christian." I know their next question will nearly always be: "What kind of Christian are you?" My reply never changes from: "I am a Christian." I don't blame people for asking the question: the blame lies squarely with the Church. We portray a Christ to the world that misrepresents Christ, and – dare I say it – presents a false Christ. Thus their question is justified. We call ourselves *born again Christians* to differentiate ourselves from those who call themselves Christians but deny the necessity of the new birth. We label ourselves *Bible-believing Christians* to make the distinction between ourselves and those who call themselves Christians but who deny the inerrancy of the Bible. We use descriptions such as Charismatic, Evangelical, Reformed, Baptist, Anglican, Pentecostal, Non-Denominational, Free, Episcopalian, Calvinist, Independent, Lutheran, Methodist. We have Reverends, Archbishops, Moderators, Cardinals, Canons, Ecumenical Patriarchs and Vicars. We don't just have pastors, we have Founding Pastors, Associate Pastors, Worship Pastors and, of course, Senior Pastors. (A pastor is an Ephesians 4 gift of Christ who shepherds God's flock; it is not a hierarchical title reserved for the leader of a Church). In some circles we even have First Ladies! The list of different kinds of Christians, along with the unbiblical titles of leaders is endless; they are an indictment of the Church and what is more, a terrible misrepresentation of the Lord Jesus Christ. Often when I share my faith with unbelievers they say they are at a loss to understand these labels we put on ourselves. They find it confusing and often justify their negative view of Christianity by asserting that despite our message of love, forgiveness and reconciliation, we are divisive and just as hostile to each other as those we seek to win to Jesus.

Their criticisms and accusations of hypocrisy are too near the knuckle to be ignored.

The New Testament knows nothing of such ludicrous titles as I have described above. The Scriptures know nothing about any kind of Christian but a Christian. Some might think I am being unnecessarily contentious, or that I am unrealistic or idealistic. Nevertheless I believe that before Jesus returns in glory the form of the Church will continue to change drastically as the restoration of all things progresses, to become the Church of God's original and ultimate intention. The true Elijah People have no interest in sustaining or prolonging denominational labels and attitudes. They seek only to be the Church that represents the Lord Jesus. The Church does not exist to make a difference; it exists to be the difference that is Jesus Christ. Bryn Jones said: "God intends a post-denominational Church to fill the world with his glory."

No more denominations

Some theologians and Church leaders advocate that such denominational descriptions that I have mentioned are good and necessary because they affirm our distinctive theologies. I am well aware of Church history and why these titles and descriptions arose and stuck. I know and appreciate the stories of how courageous men and women suffered and struggled against violent oppression and persecution for the sake of the truth they held. I have already referred to the immense courage of the Anabaptists; I admire these saints of the past and the sacrifices they made in order for us to be free to practise our faith. We are indebted to them. The seventeenth-century radical believers who subsequently became

Baptists and Congregationalists were themselves labelled Non-Conformists by their opponents because they refused to accept the legitimacy and teaching of the Established Church – the Church of England – in this country. I do not wish to downplay or insult the faith of incredibly brave believers of former times; they paid a massive price for their revelation. Many of them would be appalled by what exists today and is perpetuated in their name. These men and women were restorers, not creators or maintainers of denominational systems.

We cannot justify the continued existence and acceptance of denominationalism and redundant religious monoliths. If we have seen the restored Church, the city of God, the Bride of Christ, the mature Body of Christ, we must abandon what have become monuments to God's past activities so that we can then embrace his original and ultimate intention for the Church. The Church is diverse, but it is not denominational. We should not confuse denominations and religious traditions with the Church. Denominationalism essentially and primarily is not a Church description, a label or theological distinction; it is an attitude. The Church in a city like New York is distinct from the Church in a remote village in Vietnam. The Church in Havana, Cuba is distinct from the Church in Hamburg, Germany. The distinction is not denominational: the distinction is diversity. There is the Church in a city and the Church in a village, and everything in between. There is the Church of believers who live in the Caribbean; there is the Church of believers who live in northern Europe. But wherever you go, you meet the same people: Christians. That is what makes the Church unique: no matter where you go you see Jesus manifested in his Body on earth.

The Church worldwide is not monochrome; it will reflect to varying degrees the nation it is situated in, and even the culture of that nation. There is nothing intrinsically wrong with that. But when any natural or national culture clashes with the culture of the kingdom of God, that culture has to give way. I have worshipped God in British and Norwegian Churches, Polish and Slovakian Churches, Canadian and Malawian Churches, Russian and American Churches, Indian and South African Churches. Each one is distinct in certain regards, but the same Jesus is present in each one of them, and he demonstrates his life through them. The Churches I have mentioned do not see themselves as anything but Christians; their worship and witness reflect that fact. In the worldwide Church of Jesus Christ even national and racial boundaries have no place. The Church I am part of here in Cardiff, Wales currently has over twenty-eight different nationalities. We are not a Welsh Church or a multi-cultural Church: we are the Church. If we insist on describing the Church with additional prefixes or denominational tags that reflect religious traditions or theological preferences, we have either misunderstood or never grasped God's intention for the Church. We also have not grasped the essential nature and purpose of the Church. The moment we put labels on the Church to describe our own theologies or doctrinal stances or our revelations, we condemn ourselves as less than God's restoration people. We thus deny our identity as the Elijah People.

Just a Christian

I am not advocating that we forsake the word Christian. Far from it: it is a Bible word and one that should be recaptured without all the other adjectives we insist on prefacing it with. It is true we have a mission to explain and make things clear to the world; but I fail to understand why we insist on calling ourselves any description besides Christian. As I have just said and want to reiterate, when people ask me what kind of Christian I am, I answer I am a Christian. I can see the cogs in their brains trying to categorise me, but I refuse to be put into any of their accepted criteria. As they ask me question after question it enables me to draw them in and to tear down their deeply held conclusions on what Christianity is, what the Church is, and most important, who Jesus really is.

I will often say to people, "I'm a Christian, but I have never gone to Church in my life." It gives me an opportunity to explain that the Church is not something to which we go, the Church is who we are. Never call a building a Church! The Church is people, not bricks and stained glass windows. We are living in a time when we have to shatter the world's view that Christians are insipid, mindless, divisive, hypocritical, sectarian and irrelevant. No. We are Christians, the Church. And before the world sees Jesus come again in the clouds of glory it will see him in glory in his Church on earth.

Jesus is Lord

Let me personalise further this question of our identity as the Elijah People. There is a description and definition of Christians in the New Testament that specifically echoes Elijah's name *Yahweh is my God*. It is the life-transforming declaration: *Jesus is Lord*. These three words – Jesus is Lord – define Christianity:

God has made this Jesus, whom you crucified, both Lord and Christ. (Acts 2:36)

If you confess with your mouth that Jesus is Lord, and believe in your heart that God raised him from the dead, you will be saved. (Romans 10:9)

No one can say, "Jesus is Lord" except by the Holy Spirit. (1 Corinthians 12:3)

A Christian is someone who has received Jesus as Lord. It is that simple, yet it changes everything. A Christian is a person who has a new identity:

I have been crucified with Christ and I no longer live, but Christ lives in me. The life I now live in the body, I live by faith in the Son of God, who loved me and gave himself for me. (Galatians 2:20)

Confession of Jesus as Lord must be accompanied by personal faith in him, a faith that confesses that he died on the Cross to take away all your old sinful nature; that he rose from the dead and is alive today and has made you a brand new creation. Receiving Jesus as your Lord means you submit your whole life to him as your God, your Ruler, your Master and your Owner. Jesus claimed to be Yahweh, the *I AM WHO I AM*, the God of Abraham who appeared to Moses in the burning bush (Exodus 3:1-22). In one of the most important verses in the Bible, Jesus astounded his hearers with this claim: *"Before Abraham was born, I am!"* (John 8:58).

To say that Jesus is Lord, therefore, is the same as saying that Jesus is God; he is more than your boss, he is your God. That is why he is your Ruler, your Master and your Owner. To say that Jesus is Lord includes all these elements, but first of all he is your God. Some time ago

I was speaking on the Lordship of Jesus and thought it would be a good idea to make a list of all the things of which Jesus is Lord. I started out well; but after an hour of writing I concluded what an idiotic thing that was to do. I was writing a list that would never end. I threw the list away. Jesus is Lord of everybody and everything; nothing and no one in all creation is excluded from his Lordship. He is Lord of every life, and every moment of every life, every thought, every word and every decision of every life. Jesus is the only way, not one way among many, or just another option from which to choose.

There is an old adage that preachers sometimes use: I admit that in the past I have used it myself. It says, *Jesus is Lord of all or he is not Lord at all.* I no longer believe that. Jesus *is* Lord of all, even if I do not acknowledge his Lordship. The writer Aldous Huxley once said, "Facts do not cease to exist because they are ignored." Jesus is Lord: fact. People may not like that fact or they choose to live as if the fact is not true. Jesus is still Lord. He is also the Lord of every person who does not believe in him; he *is* Lord of all. Sometimes Christians are exhorted by preachers to make Jesus their Lord. I have heard them say, "You have received Jesus as your Saviour but now he invites you to make him your Lord." That is totally incorrect. We do not make Jesus anything, especially our Lord. Jesus is Lord because he is Lord. Jesus does not exist for *our* sake; we were created for *his* sake. Paul expresses it thus:

The Son is the image of the invisible God, the firstborn over all creation. For by him all things were created: things in heaven and on earth, visible and invisible, whether thrones or powers or rulers or *authorities; <u>all things have been created through him</u> <u>and for him</u>. He is before all things, and in him all things hold together. And he is the head of the body, the Church; he is the beginning and the firstborn from among the dead, so that in everything he might have the supremacy. (Colossians 1:15-18)*

For the Elijah People to appreciate our true identity and live to our full potential as God intends, a major shift has to take place in our thinking, and in the way we live. Christianity is not primarily about our self-fulfilment and satisfaction, the meeting of our needs, identifying our personal gifts and ministries, or working out our own visions and plans. It is not even essentially about the forgiveness of our sins and going to heaven, important as those things are. If Christ remains only a little personal Saviour to us, looking after our little lives while we remain the centre of our little universe, we are in for a rude awakening. We must know him in his fullness. Jesus did not die to manage a kindergarten; he died to reap a family of mature sons of God. Jesus did not come to this earth to fulfil our personal agendas and give us ministries, titles or positions. He did not come so we can live half-converted, dipping our toes into his life whenever we need a pick me up or to be rescued from our latest sinful rebellion and stupidity. Much that passes for Christianity today in the west is nothing more than self-absorbed and self-indulgent religion masquerading in the guise of freedom of the Spirit. Jesus called men and women to follow him; and that life begins for us on the Cross - the place where we die. Christianity is all about the centrality and supremacy of Jesus the Lord in everything:

We were never intended to be the centre of the universe – to be God. If you try to be God, to organise life around yourself as God, you run against the grain of the universe. The universe won't back your being God. So you are frustrated. You are made to belong – to belong to the King. Seek Him first and all these things will be added to you; seek yourself first and everything, including yourself, will be subtracted from you. (E. Stanley Jones)

The Living Lord

Earlier I mentioned that for Elijah the challenge he posed was not one of a choice of theologies or philosophies. For him the issue was that Yahweh was the God who lives, and who must therefore be worshipped and served. That is the same issue for us today as the Elijah People. Jesus is Lord because Jesus is alive as Lord. God the Father raised him from the dead and gave him the name above every other name:

At the name of Jesus every knee should bow, in heaven and on earth and under the earth, and every tongue confess that Jesus Christ is Lord, to the glory of God the Father. (Philippians 2:10-11)

The constant theme of the early Church was the glorious fact that Jesus is alive (see Acts 2:24; 3:15; 10:40; 13:30). They were resurrection people, bombarding their world with the wonderful news that Jesus of Nazareth, who had died on the Cross, had risen from the dead, and had ascended into heaven was now present and active on the earth in the Person of God the

Holy Spirit. The Elijah People are resurrection people! The message of the Church in every age is of a living Lord, not a dead Saviour. We do not present Jesus as one among many other options for people to choose from or as an example to follow. Jesus is the unique living Lord of all and who can be known personally. No other god lives; they are merely the inventions of Satan or the imaginings of sinful mankind.

What about me?

One day Jesus met a young man who was extremely rich (see Matthew 19:16-22). He asked Jesus what he had to do to inherit eternal life. Jesus' reply shook the young man to his core; it also had a tremendous impact on the disciples. Jesus told the young man he had to sell all he had, give the money to the poor, and then follow Jesus. This was too much for the man. Jesus highlighted his issue: he had broken the first Commandment: *you will have no other gods beside me* (Exodus 20:3). The man's particular god was his money; it was his Lord. He would not surrender his life to the Lord Jesus while he had another god, the god Money (Luke 16:13). He walked away sad; what is more significant is that Jesus let him go, even though he loved him. Jesus would not compromise his own Lordship, or submit it to the young man's Lord - Money. Jesus does not play second fiddle to anyone or anything else. Not surprisingly, the disciples were somewhat startled and disturbed by what they had just witnessed. Peter's subsequent response was a question that exposed his heart: *"We have left everything to follow you. What will there be for us?"* (Matthew 19:27).

On the surface it seems a noble question: "Lord, we've left our homes and jobs for you. We've given you everything. We've put you before our families. We've said goodbye to our reputations and home comforts. It's cost us all that we have to follow you. What do we get out of it?" This attitude is typical of many Christians: "What's in it for me? What about me? What benefit do I get from being a Christian? Lord, what can you do for me? I've given you everything; what do I get in return for following you?" Let me affirm that there are benefits from being a Christian: amazing and eternal benefits. But we do not serve Jesus for the benefits of what he does for us or what he can give us: we serve him because he is Lord.

I call this attitude the profit motive; E. Stanley Jones described it as the un-surrendered self. Note what Peter said: "We have left every *thing*." The disciples had surrendered their things to Jesus but they had not yet surrendered *themselves* to him. It is possible to call yourself a Christian, surrender everything to Jesus, yet still not surrender yourself to him as Lord. People surrender everything to Jesus except themselves. The Elijah People are different: they have surrendered themselves to Jesus. Watchman Nee wrote: "When the Lord Jesus died on the Cross he not only bore your sins away, he bore *you* away too."

At the close of World War II, the German Armed Forces surrendered to the Allies. They laid down their weapons because they had lost the war. However, many of them never surrendered themselves: in their hearts they remained Nazis for the rest of their lives. Their hearts never changed. They lived the lifestyle of respectable German citizens but their hearts always remained loyal to the Nazi cause. They had an un-surrendered self. Christians can live like that. You can live a Christian lifestyle, do the right Christian things, read your Bible every day, belong to a Church and even serve the Lord in ministry. However, your heart never surrenders to Jesus as Lord. Jesus does not want your unconditionally surrendered *things*: he wants the unconditionally surrendered *you*. Keith Green, the prophetic radical, memorably sang:

> To obey is better than sacrifice;
> I don't need your money, I want your life.

The big question

A few weeks after his resurrection Jesus went for a walk by the Sea of Galilee with Peter. It was a walk that changed Peter's life. Previously, he had denied knowing Jesus, despite promising that he never would. He had tried to kill a man when Jesus was arrested in Gethsemane. He had spent three days in abject despair after Jesus' death, convinced his own life was over. He had also doubted that Jesus was alive, even though he had seen the empty tomb and Jesus' grave clothes. By any stretch of the imagination, Peter had had a traumatic time. Yet he had come through all these things; now Jesus wanted to speak to him. As they walked together, Jesus asked Peter the big question that is the issue of Lordship: *"Do you love me more than these?"* (John 21:15).

The Bible does not tell us what the *these* were. Jesus might have been indicating the things around them: perhaps it was the fishing boats and nets that had been Peter's life and livelihood; his family and friends; the houses and streets of his village in the distance; the clothes he wore; the money in his pocket. I am glad that we do not know what the *these* were, because in reality they encompass everything. Jesus asked Peter, as he asks us, "Do you love me more than anybody and anything else?" If Jesus is your Lord – and he is – then your answer is an unequivocal yes.

Jesus is Lord, but he is not a tyrant. He loves us, and proved it by laying down his life for us. The Christian who continually questions or doubts whether God loves him needs a reality check and should grow up. My son is now an adult; he no longer asks me if I love him. I tell him that I love him and constantly demonstrate my love to him; he lives in the reality of my love. God loves you; accept it and live in the good of it. The Father's gift of his only Son was the greatest act of love in the history of the world. Furthermore, Jesus exercises his Lordship as One who loves his servants. He said that we call him Lord, but he calls us his friends:

"Greater love has no one than this: to lay down one's life for one's friends. You are my friends if you do what I command. I no longer call you servants, because a servant does not know his master's business. Instead, I have called you friends, for everything that I learned from my Father I have made known to you." (John 15:13-15)

Here is the essence of Lordship. You do what Jesus commands as your Lord and he treats you as his friend. But he cannot be your friend unless he is first of all your Lord. And you cannot be his friend if you are not first of all his servant. That order never changes. Mary, Jesus' mother, encapsulated the essential quality of his Lordship. It happened when Jesus changed the water into wine at the wedding in Cana. Before Jesus acted, Mary went to the servants and told them: "*Whatever he tells you to do, do it*" (John 2:5).

The miracle was successful not only because of Jesus' ability to perform it, but also because of the servants' unquestioning and immediate obedience to his commands. When people wonder why the Church is sometimes spiritually impotent, the problem is nothing to do with Jesus' ability as Lord: he is quite capable of performing miracles, sign and wonders. Perhaps it is more to do with the fact that we refuse to obey him as Lord because of our fear, our unbelief, our unwillingness to stand up and be counted, our apathy, our cynicism or our bitterness. The Elijah People do whatever our Lord tells us, no matter what. The outcome of our obedience is world-changing. The obedient person is a powerful tool in the hands of God. God can do anything through an obedient servant.

Lordship: the original and ultimate intention

Lordship has always been God's original and ultimate intention for humanity. Adam was created to live under God's Lordship and, together with Eve, was designed and destined to fill the earth with a people in the image of God who would express that Lordship. Adam failed because he decided that he would prefer to live free from God's rule and influence. He wanted to think and act independently of his Lord who created him. He wanted to make his own decisions, form his own values, and direct and determine his own destiny. He was desperate to define himself and not be limited to how God saw him. Therefore, he and Eve deliberately disobeyed God and ate the forbidden fruit. The results of that decision were cosmically devastating. That is what sin does; it is abnormal and goes against all that God intends for his world. We were never meant to be sinners; that was never God's original intention for us. We were and are intended to live under the loving Lordship of God through his Obedient Son in the power of God the Holy Spirit. Jesus stands in total contrast to Adam, as do all who are in Christ and who have surrendered to his Lordship:

For just as through the disobedience of the one man [Adam] the many were made sinners, so also through the obedience of the one man [Jesus] the many will be made righteous. (Romans 5:19)

We are individually and corporately designed to live under the Lordship of Jesus as Christians: that is what the Elijah People are like. All we desire together is the glory and pleasure of our Lord. We live as individuals and together as his Church exclusively for his fame and honour. We all exist solely to love and serve him; to worship him and to extend his Kingdom on earth; to tell the world that he loves them and died and rose again to be their Lord too. Together we exhibit his resurrection life. Our corporate identity as the Elijah People causes us to focus on Jesus rather than our individual selves. We live motivated and energised by this truth:

And he [God the Father] made known to us the mystery of his will according to his good pleasure, which he purposed in Christ, to be put into effect when the times will have reached their fulfilment—

to bring all things in heaven and on earth together under one head, even Christ. (Ephesians 1:9-10)

The challenge to the Church today concerning our identity as the Elijah People is the same challenge that Elijah set before the people of God at Mount Carmel that momentous day:

"How long will you limp along, hesitating and wavering between two opinions? If Yahweh is God, serve him; but if Baal, serve him." (1Kings 18:21)

FIVE

Restored Sons

The creation waits in eager expectation for the sons of God to be revealed. (Romans 8:19)

Restoration is personal and practical; it is not a hopelessly optimistic, impractical theological theory. The Elijah People are those who are being personally restored to God's original and ultimate intention for them. The Church that is being restored are real people who are being restored in every aspect of their lives.

Elijah's restoration

Elijah experienced his own personal restoration. After the highpoint of his vindication at the victory at Mount Carmel, he faced severe, violent opposition and death threats from Jezebel, which rapidly took him to rock bottom. He spiraled down from the dizzy heights of success to the depths of despair. Elijah was afraid and ran for his life. He fled south, travelling over one hundred miles (160 kilometres) to get as far away from danger as possible. He ended up in the desert, disconsolate and depressed. His life was at a low ebb. He even prayed that he might die: "*I have had enough, Yahweh. Take my life. I am no better than my ancestors*" (1Kings 19:4).

Thankfully, God refused to give up on Elijah; his grace would not let Elijah go. God sent him an angel, who provided food and drink for Elijah, despite the fact he was in the wrong place at the wrong time with the wrong attitude. Nevertheless, even after God's gracious kindness to him, Elijah went further away from God's plan for his life and kept heading south, until he came to Horeb, the mountain of God. This was the place where God had met Moses hundreds of years previously in the burning bush. It was where Moses had experienced his own personal restoration after fleeing Egypt as a young man forty years earlier. Elijah went into a cave and hid. God met him at the cave and asked him a question: *"What are you doing here, Elijah?"* (1Kings 19:9). God's purpose for Elijah was not the cave; God had a glorious future planned for him. Some people think Elijah's life ended in failure here, that he never fully recovered after running away from Jezebel in fear. That is not true; he was restored. Three aspects of his subsequent life bear this out.

First: God told Elijah to go back the way he had come to the cave because he had more for Elijah to achieve (1Kings 19:15). God spoke positively to Elijah about his future. He had to recover, or restore, what he had lost.

Second: God gave Elijah a larger, expanded mandate and commission for his future. He told him to anoint those who would achieve God's purpose for their life. In particular, he was to anoint Elisha, who would follow on after him as a prophet in an even greater measure than Elijah (1Kings 19:16-17).

Third: Elijah's own life and ministry subsequently progressed to achieve many significant things he had not yet accomplished (this is the compensation element of restoration at work). He had to encounter Ahab and Jezebel in a new and final way (1Kings 21); he would bring judgement on Ahab's successor Ahaziah; and most significant of all, he would go up to heaven in glory in a whirlwind without dying (2Kings 1-2). And do not forget that several hundred years later Elijah appeared with Moses on the Mount of Transfiguration (Matthew 17:1-8). That is hardly failure. In fact, it is a wonderful example of the principle of personal restoration.

Restored Sons

This principle of personal restoration in the life of Elijah is mirrored in our own experience. The Fall of Adam brought humanity to a place it was never intended to be. After his act of disobedience Adam hid from God; but God knew where he was and asked him a similar question to the one he asked Elijah: *"Where are you?"* (Genesis 3:9). While it is true there was no personal restoration for Adam (or for Satan, for that matter), personal restoration is available and achievable for all who are *in Adam* – for the rest of humanity who are born in sin because of Adam's original sin. God never intended us to be sinners; he always intended us to be his sons who are like his Only Son, Jesus. Sonship is God the Father's original and ultimate intention for humanity. The Elijah People are sons of God. Let's explain this vitally important truth in detail.

Adam, the first man, was the son of God (Luke 3:38). His relationship with his Creator was one of Father and son. He was like his Father, created in his image. However, God had not created Adam for Adam's sake, or merely that God could enjoy fellowship with him. God's purpose in creating Adam was that Adam would grow to maturity in his sonship to be like God's Only Son, his Uncreated Son, the Eternal Son – Jesus. Adam could not become a god, or anything like that: he and his offspring would grow more and more into the image of God the Son as they lived in obedient fellowship with God the Father and the Holy Spirit, whom God had breathed into Adam when he formed him. God the Father's purpose for Adam and his wife Eve was that they should be fruitful and so fill the earth with a people in the image of God, a people like his Son:

> Then God said, "Let us make mankind in our image, in our likeness, so that they may rule over the fish in the sea and the birds in the sky, over the livestock and all the wild animals, and over all the creatures that move along the ground." So God created mankind in his own image, in the image of God he created them; male and female he created them. God blessed them and said to them, "Be fruitful and increase in number; fill the earth and subdue it. Rule over the fish in the sea and the birds in the sky and over every living creature that moves on the ground." (Genesis 1:26-28)

God the Father loved Jesus his Son so much he desired to fill all things with him through Adam and his offspring. God's purpose is still to have a family of sons like his Only Son. That is his original and ultimate intention for humanity. As Adam and Eve lived in obedience to God and fed from the tree of life (which is a picture of Jesus), their offspring or *seed* would be the sons of God who would fill the whole earth with the glory of God.

However, Adam's sin was catastrophic. He disobeyed his Father and consequently fell from his position of sonship. Through his wilful disobedience he threw away his destiny and became a different man with a different 'father', the devil. Another race thus came into being: whereas to be *in Adam* had meant to be like God, now it meant to be like the devil. All of Adam's offspring, all his human descendants, the rest of humanity, including each one of us, would be like him: disobedient sinners instead of obedient sons. Instead of the earth being filled with a people in the image of God, it was now being filled with another race of sinful sons like their 'father', the devil:

> *All Adam's offspring – seed – were meant to be 'sons of God' – but after sin entered they were sons of the devil, held under his dominion, his sway and control. They are like him. (E.W. Kenyon)*

Sin is a serious issue. We must never minimise, or even worse, disregard its destructive, death-inducing power. While we are no longer sinners because of our faith in Jesus, we should always appreciate with deep gratitude the awful predicament that God rescued us from. Before we met Jesus we were not good people who just needed a bit of cleaning up. We were not basically decent people who needed someone to help us. We were unrighteous sinners, rebellious towards God, totally steeped in sin and headed for eternity spent in hell. We had all fallen way short of God's glorious, holy standard (Romans 3:23). Have you ever considered how sin affects God? It cost him the life of his Son to eradicate it from your life. R.A. Torrey said: "God's love to sinners will never be appreciated until seen in the light of his blazing wrath at sin."

No change

Despite all the havoc, the cosmic damage and chaos Adam had caused through his sinful disobedience, God's purpose remained, and still remains, the same. Even in that moment of sinful disobedience in Eden, God was prepared. He promised the devil that his evil plan would fail:

"I will put enmity between you and the woman, and between your offspring and hers; he will crush your head, and you will strike his heel." (Genesis 3:15)

God promised that a man would be born into this world, the Seed or Offspring of the Woman, who would 'crush the head' of the devil. In that act of crushing the man would experience terrible suffering, but in that suffering would triumph over the devil. It is interesting that Jesus was crucified at Golgotha, which means *Place of the Skull*. The moment he was lifted up on the Cross and died, he victoriously and once for all crushed the devil's head!

Isaiah prophesied about a man who would come to take away the sin of the world. In one of the most famous chapters in the Bible, Isaiah said of this man who would suffer and die for us: *He will see his offspring and prolong his days* (Isaiah 53:10). The One who would be wounded for our transgressions and bruised for our iniquities would, in that act of self-sacrifice and death, produce many offspring – many sons – for God the Father. We must always remember that the Cross of Christ was no freakish accident or the plan of the devil. It was God's own pre-planned solution for sin and the means by which the Father could sow his Only Son in order to reap a whole family of sons:

In bringing many sons to glory, it was fitting that God, for whom and through whom everything exists, should make the author of their salvation perfect through suffering. Both the one who makes men holy and those who are made holy are of the same family. So Jesus is not ashamed to call them brothers. (Hebrews 2:10-11)

Two races

There now exists two races, two kinds of people: those *in Adam* and those *in Christ*. Those in Adam are sinners who have not received Jesus as Lord; those in Christ are Christians – the Elijah People. A.W. Tozer called these two races the once-born and the twice-born. The New Testament makes this contrast quite clear: Jesus himself said to those who opposed him and denied his claims to be God and the Lord of all, that they were of their father – the devil (John 8:44). Paul also contrasted Adam and Jesus, stating that those in Christ are like Christ:

The first man Adam became a living being; the last Adam, a life-giving spirit. The spiritual did not come first, but the natural, and after that the spiritual. The first man was of the dust of the earth, the second man from heaven. As was the earthly man, so are those who are of the earth; and as is the man from heaven, so also are those who are of heaven. And just as we have borne the likeness of the earthly man, so let us bear the likeness of the man from heaven. (1Corinthians 15:45-49)

DeVern Fromke explains it thus:

God not only speaks of the first and last Adam, but also of the first and second man...When the Lord Jesus was crucified on the Cross, He was nailed there and laid in the tomb as the last Adam. All that was in the first Adam was gathered up and done away in Him. In God's reckoning, Adam was left in the grave. We were included there. By Jesus' death the old race was completely wiped out...There will never be another Adam. When Christ, as the last Adam, had moved into death, He had carried a whole family into the grave, and over it God had pronounced: The End! But Christ, as the second Man, brought forth a new race by his resurrection.

Christians are no longer in Adam. That means nothing of our old sinful nature exists anymore; we are new creations in Christ (2Corinthians 5:17). We now have the righteous nature of Christ himself. All that Adam lost through his sinful act we recover in our new birth when we become children of God – complete righteousness and holiness. This is the beginning of our personal restoration. We become what we were always intended to be – as righteous as Jesus:

You were taught, with regard to your former way of life, to put off your old self, which is being corrupted by its deceitful desires; to be made new in the attitude of your minds; and to put on the new self, created to be like God in true righteousness and holiness. (Ephesians 4:22-24)

Children and Sons

Sonship is a major theme in the New Testament. Christians are often referred to as children and sons of God. Let me say at this point that Christian sonship is nothing to do with gender; rather, it describes our status, privileges and mature responsibility as believers. Ladies are sons of God too; the New Testament makes that clear:

You are all sons of God through faith in Christ Jesus, for all of you who were baptised into Christ have clothed yourselves with Christ. There is neither Jew nor Greek, slave nor free, male nor female, for you are all one in Christ Jesus. If you belong to Christ, then you are Abraham's seed, and heirs according to the promise. (Galatians 3:26-29)

In Christ there are no religious, racial, social or gender divides: nobody is better than anybody else. The colour of our skin or our social status makes no difference to God. Our wealth, or lack of it, means nothing to him. We are all equally sons of God through our personal faith in Jesus as Lord. Christians are children of God; we belong to God's family and God is our Father:

To all who received him, those who believed in his name, he gave the right to become children of God. (John 1:12)

How great is the love the Father has lavished on us, that we should be called children of God! And that is what we are! (1John 3:1)

The image of our being children of God emphasises our new birth: that we have been born again and, just as natural children have a childlike faith, so we have put our faith in God. Therefore, the use of the word *child* in the context of being a Christian highlights our new birth into a new creation and our new nature; our belonging to the family of God the Father; and our childlike faith in God that continues all our lives. However, to be childlike in our faith in no way implies that we continue to behave in a childish manner. That is why the New Testament also stresses that we are not only children of God, but that we are also sons of God. Romans 8:15 says we have received the Spirit of sonship or adoption (*huiothesia*, which literally means *the placing of a son*). The Greek word *huios* describes an adult, mature son, as opposed to a baby or child. *Huiothesia* was a technical term used outside the New Testament for an act that had specific, legal, permanent effects and consequences in which a slave would be adopted by his master into the family and so be put in every respect in exactly the same position and nature as any of the man's natural sons. In reality, he became a birth son and possessed the same name, rights, identity, standing, citizenship and inheritance as any of the man's natural sons. He became a true son of his adoptive father. He also had the same responsibilities and obligations as his brothers. He now lived for his father and the rest of his brothers. He was no longer a slave but a son. He had a new identity and all the privileges and responsibilities which accompanied that new identity.

Mature Sons

Our sonship as Christians, therefore, is to do with our maturity. The New Testament concept of mature sonship is the compensation dimension of our personal restoration as the Elijah People. We as the children of God grow to become his mature sons:

Therefore, brothers, and sisters we have an obligation and responsibility—but it is not to the flesh, to live according to it and be controlled by it. For if you live according to the flesh, you will surely die; but if by the power of the Spirit within you, you practically put to death the misdeeds of the body, you will live, because those whose way of life is the Spirit of God are sons of God. (Romans 8:12-14 author's translation)

The whole creation waits in eager expectation and longing for us, the sons of God, to be revealed. It is standing on tiptoe, straining in anticipation to see the wonderful sight of the mature sons of God coming into their own. (Romans 8:19 author's translation, with thanks to J.B. Phillips)

We also know beyond doubt that in everything that happens God works for the good of those who love him, who have been called according to his eternal purpose. Every one of those men and women God the Father foreknew from eternity, he also predestined before the beginning of time to be conformed to the likeness of his Son, that they would be just like Jesus, so that Jesus might be the firstborn among many brothers, the eldest of a family of sons. And those God the Father eternally predestined to be his sons, he also called to be his sons; those he called, he also justified, making them holy and righteous in his sight. Those he justified, he also glorified, raising them to a heavenly condition and dignity, filling them with his glorious splendour. (Romans 8:28-30 author's translation)

The Holy Spirit indwells us in order to produce maturity, to make us conform more and more to the likeness of Jesus. The major emphasis regarding sonship in the New Testament is that we achieve maturity, fullness and completion as sons: that is the Spirit's work in us. His role is to so perfectly form Christ in us that together as the Elijah People we become the mature corporate man, the sons of God, whose appearing the creation eagerly awaits. This is a key aspect of the restoration of all things. That is why sonship and maturity are contrasted with childishness and immaturity:

*It was he [Christ] who gave some to be apostles, some to be prophets, some to be evangelists, and some to be pastors and teachers, to prepare God's people for works of service, so that the body of Christ may be built up until we all reach unity in the faith and in the knowledge of the Son of God and become **mature**, attaining to the whole **measure of stature** of the **fullness** of Christ. Then we will no longer be **infants**, tossed back and forth by the waves, and blown here and there by every wind of teaching and by the cunning and craftiness of men in their deceitful scheming. Instead, speaking the truth in love, we will in all things grow up into him who is the Head, that is, Christ.*

From him the whole body, joined and held together by every supporting ligament, grows and builds itself up in love, as each part does its work. (Ephesians 4:11-16)

This brings us to the heart of this matter of our personal restoration as the Elijah People. Remember that Elijah continued to progress in his life to the place where he did not see death but went to heaven in the whirlwind. He grew in maturity until he was ready to enter the glory of heaven. This is an illustration of the maturity or completion of the Elijah People. Let me explain quite clearly: I am not advocating that it is possible for Christians to enter heaven now without death. The New Testament makes it very clear that until Jesus returns we will all die. No: this illustration shows us that the Church as the Elijah People will grow in its maturity as the sons of God to the state in which it so demonstrates and manifests Jesus the Son in all his fullness that the restoration of all things will be complete and he will return to usher in the new age. There will be a mature generation of the Elijah People that will be alive when Jesus returns and who will not see physical death (1Thessalonians 4:13-18). Why can't that generation be us?

You will notice that I have highlighted several key words in the passage from Ephesians quoted above. Each one of them is vitally important in the practical outworking of this process to mature sonship of the Elijah People: they all apply to every Christian. We cannot speak of the Church without speaking of those who are the Church: real people, you and me. Our personal lives are lives that must be personally restored. Each one of us must grow to maturity in our sonship. We all have to become in our individual lives what God wants for us so that together in our corporate life as the Elijah People we will grow to our corporate mature sonship and hasten the return of Jesus. Let's look at these highlighted words so they can help us understand what is required of each of us as sons of God.

Mature

In the New Testament this word (*teleios*) means completion; perfection; a consummated goal; maturity; conclusion. It means to go through all the necessary stages of a journey and reach the end goal or destination. When describing how we must live as Christians it is often translated as *perfect*, to convey this sense of ever-increasing maturity in our faith, revelation, attitudes and behaviour:

> *Be perfect, therefore, as your heavenly Father is perfect. (Matthew 5:48)*

> *All of us who are mature [perfect] should take such a view of things. (Philippians 3:15)*

> *We proclaim him, admonishing and teaching everyone with all wisdom, so that we may present everyone perfect in Christ. (Colossians 1:28)*

Measure

The word *measure* (*metron*) means a standard, or the basis for determining what is fair or sufficient. A standard was the controlling factor by which things were determined to be acceptable, correct or true. Jesus used it to describe the attitude of our hearts when we give:

"Give, and it will be given to you. A good measure, pressed down, shaken together and running over, will be poured into your lap. For with the measure you use, it will be measured to you." (Luke 6:38)

The English word metronome comes from this Greek word. A metronome is used by musicians to practise keeping a piece of music at a regular, consistent pace or tempo. Jesus is our metronome: he determines the pace or tempo of our lives. As a musician will practise a piece slower than he will eventually perform it, increasing the tempo set by the metronome in stages, so the Spirit of Jesus in us continually stretches, transforms and matures us so that we become more and more who we really are as the Elijah People. Jesus, therefore, is the perfect standard by which we determine everything: our maturity or perfection is nothing less than attaining to all he expects and demands of us: full sonship. Jesus is the perfect standard by which we measure everything else. He is *the* Way, *the* Truth and *the* Life (John 14:6). Jesus sets the pace and tempo of our 'growing up into him who is the Head' (Ephesians 4:15).

Stature

Many of the English translations omit this important word (*helikia*); but it is in the Greek text. It means *full-aged* or the end stage of a lifespan. Like the word *teleios* it also means mature, but has the added connotation of attaining stature and dignity, not merely growing up in years or growing older. It is used of Jesus to describe how he grew from a twelve-year old boy to a man: *Jesus grew in wisdom and stature, and in favour with God and men* (Luke 2:52). Jesus did not only change physically from a baby to a child to a man: he also grew in stature to manhood and manliness. He became a man not only physically but also in his character and his attitudes. We will discuss this further in due course.

Fullness

This word (*pleroma*) is very important. It means to be full; to be filled to over-full, to fulfil or complete. The word was used to describe a fully laden ship. We might use it to describe how we feel after eating too much food: "I am full to bursting!" The word describes a fullness or perfection in quantity and quality:

The Word became flesh and made his dwelling among us. We have seen his glory, the glory of the One and Only, who came from the Father, full [richly full] of grace and truth. (John 1:14)

For in Christ all the fullness of the Deity lives in bodily form, and you have been given fullness in Christ, who is the head over every power and authority. (Colossians 2:9-10)

God placed all things under his feet and appointed him to be head over everything for the Church, which is his body, the fullness of him who fills everything in every way. (Ephesians 1:22-23)

[I pray] that you may be filled with all the fullness of God. (Ephesians 3:19)

These verses show us that Jesus himself is the fullness of God; that in his life on earth he fully demonstrated the life of God; that Christians also are now filled with all the fullness of God through the Holy Spirit in us; and that together as the Elijah People we increasingly live out and demonstrate this fullness of Christ corporately as the Church.

Infant

This word (*nepios*) is different from the New Testament word used to describe our relationship to God as his children. This particular term described an infant child, or one who was immature. It was also used to describe those adults who were childish in their attitudes and behaviour: those who behaved in an infantile, irresponsible, immature fashion. Paul accused the Corinthian Church of this unacceptable behaviour:

Brothers, I could not address you as spiritual but as worldly—mere infants in Christ. (1 Corinthians 3:1)

When maturity comes, immaturity goes. When I was infantile, I spoke in an infantile way; I thought and set my mind with an infantile attitude; I considered everything in an infantile way. When I grew to be a man I was done with being infantile; that way of living was totally gone from my life. (1 Corinthians 13:10-11, author's translation)

On to maturity

The heart cry of God the Father is for his children to grow up to sonship, to leave our infantile, immature, self-centred and selfish ways behind us and become the mature sons of God we were always intended to be.

The matter of personal restoration is not only to do with our welfare and blessing, or with our personal fulfilment and forgiveness of sins. These things are all valid, but there is a greater agenda that God has for us: our mature sonship. The eternal immaturity of the sons of God is unthinkable. Speaking of this, T. Austin-Sparks commented:

Now, in the practical way, let us note the difference between infants, spiritually, called children in the New Testament, and sons. The difference is simply this, that infants or children have everything done for them and they live in the good of that for which they themselves have had no exercise. That is the difference. An infant is one who lives on the good of other people's exercise and has never had any exercise for itself. Everything has been done and prepared for it… nothing has been done by the child itself… But a son, in the scriptural and spiritual sense, is one who is… progressively coming out of the realm where everything is done for him… to the place where… he is becoming one who is competent in himself, and no longer dependent upon what others do and say. Everything is not being brought ready made to him. There is a sense in which it is being made in him and he is making it in his own experience by the exercise of his own senses.

Paul said that when he became a man he was done with being infantile: that way of living was totally gone from his life – he had to put his childish ways behind him (1Corinthians 13:11). That phrase means to *render something inoperative*, to take something out of the sphere of operation so that it no longer has an effect and does not apply anymore. In the restoration plan of God for his Church it is time for the Elijah People to grow up 'into the Head' – to become like our elder brother and Lord. It is time to leave the childish ways of living behind us. It is time for the revealing of the sons of God. As T. Austin-Sparks so pertinently asked: "Why should maturity be so long delayed and a nursery so long occupied?"

Maturity is a process; it is not something that we suddenly achieve when we reach, say, eighteen or sixty. There is an adage which pertinently says, 'there is no fool like an old fool'. Spiritual maturity is the same. The length of time somebody has been a Christian is not necessarily an indication of their maturity in Christ. I have met Christians in their twenties who were far more mature in Christ than others I have met who were in their seventies. Some Christians who have been saved for five years are far more spiritually mature than those who have been saved fifty years. Spiritual maturity is all to do with the process of growing up as obedient sons in our sense of identity and in our relationship with God the Father in the power of the Holy Spirit. Let me practicalise this idea of growing to maturity as sons of God; let's see some of the childish ways that have to be put behind us if we are going to attain to mature sonship as the Elijah People.

Attitude

Your attitude should be the same as that of Christ Jesus. (Philippians 2:5)

Children live for themselves; they inhabit a small world that revolves exclusively around them. Children are essentially self-centred. They must be taught that there is a greater world than them and that they cannot be the focus and centre of everything. Any parent will agree that it does not take long for this self-centredness to become apparent: put two children in a room with one toy and see what happens. Children throw tantrums or sulk when they do not get their own way. They have to be taught how to behave, how to share. They have to learn that life is not all about them. The attitude of a child is childish! It is not the attitude of an adult. When I became a man I could not behave with the attitudes I had when I was a child; they had to go. As I grew up I learned that I had to change; my attitudes had to become those of a grown up. I am now a father and have children of my own; they too are now adults, and my son is himself a father. Imagine what my children would think of me if, for example, I sulked or moaned because I did not get what I wanted for Christmas. They would say to me, "Dad, act your age. Grow up!"

My daughter Naomi is a schoolteacher; her class comprises four and five year olds. When Naomi was their age her own attitude and behaviour were exactly like the children she now teaches. Imagine if she still had the same attitudes now as those little kids: it would be disastrous! Even more seriously: Naomi would not be able to function as a teacher if she had the same attitudes as the children in her class. She would be disqualified. If a child disobeys or throws a tantrum or sulks, Naomi cannot respond in the same way. She cannot throw her book on the floor and stomp her feet because the children fail do what she wants. She has to behave as an adult; she has grown to maturity, so she is qualified not only in her academic ability but also as a person to do her job. She has left her childish ways behind; they no longer operate in her life. Her personal maturity is just as important as her academic qualification and ability to teach.

The sons of God, the Elijah People, do not live with selfish or self-centred attitudes. Their focus is not on themselves. We already spoke of this in the previous chapter: the Elijah People live with the attitude of maturity in which they discover that life is not about them but about their Lord and elder brother Jesus, and about other people. They have surrendered themselves, not only their *things*; they do not live for themselves but for others. Paul put it like this: *Love does not insist on its own way* (1Corinthians 13:5). The Elijah People are, therefore, mature in their attitudes. They live by the life of Another: the Spirit of Jesus lives the life of Jesus with the mature attitude of Jesus in them.

Responsibility

"Whoever can be trusted with very little can also be trusted with much, and whoever is dishonest with very little will also be dishonest with much. So if you have not been trustworthy in handling worldly wealth, who will trust you with true riches? And if you have not been trustworthy with someone else's property, who will give you property of your own?" (Luke 16:10-12)

Don't you know we will judge angels? How much more the things of this life! (1Corinthians 6:3)

Part of the maturing process is being given personal responsibility and taking personal responsibility. When my children were little I had to run them around all over the place. They used to sit in the back of the car, 'driving' with their imaginary steering wheels. Finally the day came when they were old enough to learn to drive. They had to move out from the back seat into the driver's seat and take control of the car for themselves. I was not going to transport them around the rest of their lives. They had to learn to drive for themselves and take control of a real steering wheel; they had to take responsibility, and I had to be willing to give responsibility to them.

I distinctly remember my son James returning home after passing his driving test, full of excitement. His first words to me were, "Dad, can I borrow the car?" For a moment I panicked and hesitated: my little boy behind the wheel of my car! Then I realised he was now qualified; he could do this and I had to let him take responsibility. I handed him the keys. With that he and his sister ran from the house, dived into my car and drove off, with their parents staring after them as they disappeared around the corner. Not only was my son driving my car: his first passenger was my little girl! Now my children have their own cars and drive all over the country. They have taken responsibility for themselves.

The Elijah People take personal responsibility for their own lives. It is true that the Church is a loving community that supports, encourages and helps each other. We bear each other's burdens and share our lives. We belong to each other and care for each other. The Christian life is intrinsically and essentially corporate; but it is not merely a self-help group or a long-term spiritual nursing home for the terminally needy. Our leaders are not intended to be people who constantly wipe our noses and transport us around while we sit in the back seat with our imaginary steering wheels, playing at driving the 'car' of our lives. They are not here to micro-manage our lives or to live our lives for us. We have to take personal responsibility for ourselves.

Let me give just one example. A vital aspect of the Christian life is the discipline of regular prayer and reading the Word of God. There is an old song that says, *read your Bible, pray every day if you want to grow.* That is true. In just the same way that I have to eat a proper diet regularly if I am going to grow and remain healthy, so prayer and regular reading of the Bible are necessary for me if I am going to grow into mature sonship. There is no shortcut. I cannot piggy-back on somebody else's relationship with Jesus: I must have my own relationship with him. Regular prayer and time spent reading the Word of God are absolutely necessary for me to become mature. Nobody else can do that for me.

Elijah was a man just like us (James 5:17). I find that incredibly encouraging and challenging. He was a man who learned the place and power of prayer, especially his own personal responsibility to pray and then to act on his prayer:

He prayed earnestly that it would not rain, and it did not rain on the land for three and a half years. Again he prayed, and the heavens gave rain, and the earth produced its crops. (James 5:17-18)

Elijah learned the discipline of regular prayer; therefore his prayers were powerful and effective (James 5:16). He also took responsibility for what he prayed. It seems that too many Christians today want others to do the hard work for them or they are too busy to spend time with God in prayer and in the Bible. I remember a Godly man who told me: "If you are too busy to pray – you are too busy." Later on we will discuss the importance and centrality of the Word of God for the Elijah People and devote a chapter to the place of prayer in our corporate life; for now let me emphasise: you cannot mature as a son of God without a regular diet of personal prayer and reading the Bible. It might sound old fashioned to say so, especially in this modern world of instant gratification, shallow commitment and the emphasis on gaining easy overnight success. You must take responsibility for your own walk with God in this regard: read your Bible and pray every day if you want to grow. There is no other way.

True value

Children do not appreciate or understand the true value of things. My granddaughter Tabitha was eight months old at her first Christmas. Naturally, she was inundated with gifts. However, she was equally fascinated with the wrapping paper, and spent ages ripping it and holding it above her head! By the time she is eighteen I am certain that things will be different. When I was a child my parents owned a beautiful leather chair upholstered with buttons. One day, when I was about three or four, I became intrigued by how the buttons were fixed to the chair. So I went to the kitchen, took a sharp knife from the drawer, and proceeded to dig out the buttons. By the time my dad discovered me I had all but destroyed the chair. My own children broke ornaments and put toys in the video player when they were little; now they know better.

Mature people understand the true value of things. For the Elijah People this means we understand and appreciate increasingly the true value of what it means to be a

Christian: for example, the true value of Jesus, the purpose of the Church, the prominence and values of the kingdom of God, who we are in Christ, the centrality of the Holy Spirit. When I received Jesus as my Lord and Saviour in 1966, I did so because I did not want to go to hell. For me, Jesus was the means by which I escaped eternal punishment. One year later I was baptised in water because I wanted to obey his command. I belonged to the Church because that is what Christians do. All these things are right and valid: to reject Jesus is to be condemned to an eternal hell; we are baptised because he commands it; we belong to the Church because that is the right thing.

However, as I have grown in Christ over the years, I have gained much more appreciation of the true value of spiritual things, which are the true realities. It is not that I know more doctrine or facts about Christianity; merely knowing something does not bring appreciation of it. Maturity brings appreciation and a sense of value that determines behaviour and conduct. I do not only believe in God: I know him. Jesus is not merely my personal Lord and Saviour and ticket to heaven. I have discovered, and continue to discover, that he is the glory of God, the focus of the plan of the Father for humanity, the Head of the Church, the King of the Kingdom, the complete revelation of the Father. I understand more and more what Arthur Wallis meant when he said: "The grand design of history is to bring God's Son into the possession of his inheritance." Jesus is the centre and circumference; he is the Eternal God. He is the One that history and creation is all about:

God the Father made known to us the mystery of his will according to his good pleasure, which he purposed in Christ, to be put into effect when the times will have reached their fulfilment—to bring all things in heaven and on earth together under one head, even Christ. (Ephesians 1:9-10)

This growing sense of value continues to transform me, affecting every aspect of my existence. It increasingly determines my every thought, action, word, and motive. The Elijah People are not dry, theological experts who think they know everything, or shallow, immature children who glory in their ignorance. They are those who are being restored and transformed from one degree of glory to another degree of glory (2Corinthians 3:18), all the while growing in their revelation of God and his purpose.

The view

Every father enjoys hoisting his children on to his shoulders so they can get a better view of what is going on: the parade; the game; the band; the animals at the zoo. I did it for my kids. Now they are grown and they see for themselves. They no longer need to sit on my shoulders. They have the same view as me. Nowadays my son is taller than me so he can see even more. His view is not restricted by my eyes: he sees for himself. In fact, he can see beyond me. I have taught my children to see things for themselves: they have their own faith in Jesus, they see him for themselves. Consequently, our conversations are different from when they were young in years and in faith. They no longer seek answers to certain questions: they have established that God loves them and that he is good no matter what happens to them. They have learned for themselves the spiritual laws of sowing and reaping, that God is their source. My longing for my children is that they see more of Christ and of God's restoration purpose than I do, because that is the compensation nature of restoration. Each generation of the Elijah People moves the restoration purpose on further than the previous generation. They can do that only if they are seeing more than those who have preceded them. This is a vitally important element of restoration: if succeeding generations of the Elijah People do not advance the purpose of God further than previous generations, then the coming of the Lord Jesus is not hastened and – this can happen – what has been restored once might need to be recaptured again by future generations.

I once read an article in *Time* magazine about how languages die. Experts note three distinct stages in the process:

- A language is considered endangered when children no longer speak it.
- A language is considered moribund (about to die) when only a handful of elderly speakers are left.
- A language is extinct when there are no speakers left.

There are important lessons for us as the Elijah People in this concerning the passing on of our 'language' from one generation of faith to another. Our 'language' is our revelation of the restoration plan and purpose of God. Psalm 48:12-14 tells us to walk about Zion (the Kingdom people of God, the Church), to have a good look at her so that we can tell the next generation what we have seen and are building so they will do the same.

We see in Judges chapter two how this trans-generational impartation of revelation broke down. Verse eight of this chapter records the death of Joshua; there then follows a tragic statement: *after that whole generation had died, another generation grew up, who neither knew Yahweh nor what he had done for Israel...they did evil in the eyes of Yahweh* (Judges 2:10-11). Something terrible had happened. The previous generation of God's people failed to impart to the next generation any sense of knowing God or his restoration purpose. Their 'language' moved from being endangered, through the moribund state, to extinction. The result was that by the time the previous generation died, the next generation had no moorings to hold them. They had no root, no foundation.

Who was to blame? Not the younger generation, surely. No, the responsibility lay with the previous generation; they failed to prepare and equip their children for God's eternal purpose. There is a divine responsibility on those of us who have walked in the ways of God and his restoration purpose that our revelation does not die with us. I have a priority to give myself to impart to the younger generation of men and women of God the truth I have walked in and the vision of the restored bride that the Church is becoming. And if I die before Jesus returns, then the next generation will play their part fully in bringing him back.

As we grow in maturity as sons of God and as the Elijah People our view constantly grows. We see for ourselves, and what we have seen spurs us on. We often call it having a vision. Sometimes people ask me what keeps me going, despite the many setbacks, disappointments and failures that I have experienced. I tell them, "I have seen something." Paul was controlled and directed by what he had seen; all his life with Jesus it kept him through times of success and difficulties, so he could say: *"I was not disobedient to the vision from heaven"* (Acts 26:19). It was the same for Abraham. At the age of seventy-five, he left everything to follow what he had seen, and he spent the next hundred years living and energised by a vision:

He was looking forward to the city with foundations, whose architect and builder is God. (Hebrews 11:10)

A lifelong process

Maturity to restored sonship is a process that lasts all our lives. We are works in progress. As we arrive at the close of this chapter, let me encourage you to gauge your own increasing maturity in Christ. Consider these few things:

- Have you grown up in your attitudes? (Read Galatians 5:19-26)
- What personal responsibilities have you taken for your life?
- How often do you pray and read the Bible?
- What have you discovered about God the Father, the Lord Jesus and the Holy Spirit that you didn't realise before?
- What do you now value about the Church that you didn't before?
- What is better about your life than six months ago?
- What new adventures has Jesus spoken to you about?
- What does God demand and expect of you right now?
- Are you imparting the vision of restoration to the next generation?

SIX

Status Quo (1)

*"How long will you go limping between
two different opinions?" (1Kings 18:21)*

Elijah certainly did not live an obscure life. God
propelled him into the heart of his world, not merely to
make a difference but to *be* the difference that only a man
or woman of God can be. We cannot escape the fact that
Elijah was in some regards a confrontationalist. We have
seen that Elijah did not live in his own little world,
cocooned from what was going on around him; he did
not hide away in a religious ghetto with his own private
faith, keeping himself to himself. He was deliberately
controversial and outspoken; he provoked strong
responses and reactions from people. Early on in his story,
God sent him to Zarephath, which was the origin and
centre of worship for Baal-Melqart. While there, right in
the heart of 'enemy territory' so to speak, he performed
miracles and raised a young boy from the dead. He lived
under God's spotlight, as God's instrument, demonstrating
the life and power of Yahweh. Even when Elijah ran for his
life and ended up in the cave, God sent him back and then
onwards to even greater and significant prominence.

As you read Elijah's story you will soon discover that
he constantly challenged and confronted people and
situations: he confronted Ahab and Jezebel concerning

the way they led the nation into idolatry, and their murderous treatment of Naboth; he challenged the assumptions and unbelief of the widow at Zarephath when her son died; he confronted and overcame death itself and raised the boy from the dead; he confronted and killed the prophets of Baal-Melqart at Mount Carmel; he challenged the people not to limp along between two opinions, but to follow Yahweh; he challenged Obadiah's fears; he challenged his servant's lack of faith when he sent him to look for the rain cloud; he confronted Ahab's successor Ahaziah; he even provoked Elisha to leave the comfort and safety of his livelihood and follow him. Everywhere he went he challenged people to believe in Yahweh as their God. Sometimes Elijah was an uncomfortable person to be around or to be associated with. It seems that nobody was neutral in their opinions of Elijah. He caused either positive responses or negative reactions.

A politically incorrect prophet

Elijah would not fit into today's politically correct world, where compromise, tolerance, broad-mindedness and moderation reflect the spirit of the age. The worst thing one can do today is to offend anybody's views, especially when it comes to religion and morality. Elijah had no time for such sensitivities. Look how he taunted the prophets of Baal-Melqart at Mount Carmel when there was no response to their ranting:

Elijah mocked them, saying, "Cry aloud, for he is a god. Either he is musing, or he is relieving himself, or he is on a journey, or perhaps he is asleep and must be awakened." (1 Kings 18:27)

Elijah was not concerned about offending people! He had no time for inter-faith dialogue; he just said it like it was. He also insulted the god of the Syrians, Baal-zebul (meaning *life-god*), by calling him Baal-zebub (*lord of the flies:* see 2Kings 1:2). Jesus called the devil by this name too (Matthew 10:25). Elijah was not alone in using very strong language when confronting apostasy and hypocrisy; the prophet Amos famously called the prominent women of society 'drink-sodden fat cows' (Amos 4:1-2). Now, in no way do I advocate religious hatred or acts of violence against those who believe differently from me. We do not burn Korans or persecute people because they are of other religions or live an immoral life that is totally contrary to the Bible. Neither do we support the murder of doctors who perform abortions. We do not incite violence. The reality is that many Christians suffer terribly at the hands of other religions and political systems, but Christians do not act that way. Christians are different; in fact they are unique. Nevertheless, we have to agree with Elijah's forceful sentiment, and we must assert that there is no God besides the God of the Bible. The god of Islam does not exist; he is not Yahweh by another name. The gods of Hinduism do not exist. The Jesus of Mormonism does not exist. All religions are not of equal value. Those are not statements of hatred; they are statements of objective truth. Francis Schaeffer pertinently commented: "It is ridiculous to say that all religions teach the same things, when they disagree at the fundamental point as to what God is like." I have an acquaintance who is a devout Muslim. Whenever we meet we get on very well. When it comes to the question of whether Islam and Christianity have anything in common, we both agree that there is a vast chasm between us. He denies that Jesus is God; I believe Jesus is God. That does not cause us to fight; we both know that is the fundamental issue of truth and the core of our identity. He believes he is right and I am wrong; I know I am right and he is wrong! We don't go to war over our contrary beliefs about Jesus and God the Father. I don't burn his Koran and he doesn't burn my Bible. But we both agree that Muslims and Christians have nothing in common regarding the deity of Jesus Christ.

No common ground

Christianity has nothing in common with other religious systems or political philosophies. We love the people of this world too much not to tell them the truth: there is only one God who lives and who loves them. We do the world no favours by watering down the uniqueness of our faith, the Lordship of Jesus, and the radical exclusivity of Christianity, and then seek to find the lowest common denominator among all religions to which we can subscribe. It is a waste of time and a denial of the truth, and it is something the Old Testament prophets specifically condemned and the New Testament Church stood against, often at the cost of their lives. Jesus Christ is Lord and is the only way to God. If we discard the uniqueness of Jesus Christ as God we have nothing left. If we dilute the truth that Jesus is the only way to the only God we might as well pack up and quit. That is the challenge we face as the Elijah People. Commenting on Elijah's political incorrectness, Terry Virgo said: "The Bible is hostile to religion that isn't lined up with the authentic God."

Why did Elijah live like this, constantly challenging and provoking people and situations? Let me say at this point I do not believe he was a cantankerous man filled with bitterness and a bad temper. He was not like those people I sometimes see on the streets of my city who rant and scream at passers-by, condemning them and railing about damnation and hell-fire, even though hell is real. Elijah did not live out of hatred of people; he just lived according to a different status quo from everybody else. The controlling factor of Elijah's life was what he believed about God and what God wanted. He lived from God's desire for this world. Elijah had seen something of God's restoration purpose; therefore he would not accept anything else or anything less than God's purpose and intention. He lived according to God's status quo. Ultimately, nothing could deter or distract him from it.

God's status quo

The Elijah People also live from God's status quo; there is nothing else that captivates and motivates them. They live from the perspective of God's original and ultimate intention. They are restoration people; therefore, they will inevitably be those who challenge any status quo that opposes or settles for less than God's restoration purpose. They also easily respond to the challenges that the restoration purpose of God brings their way. They are swift to change when confronted with the practical demands of the restoration of all things on their own lives. They do not point the finger at others while ignoring what the restoration of all things requires of them. The Elijah People stand firmly against all that is against or outside of God's status quo. At the same time they are the first to change when God reveals more of his restoration purpose and what it means for them personally. The Elijah People are pioneers, not settlers.

As I have previously mentioned: I was raised a Baptist. My parents were Baptists; my mother's parents were Baptists. We were also called Evangelicals, which meant that I was taught to believe the Bible is the Word of God. I am glad I was taught that truth: the Bible is the fully inspired Word of God. I believe the Bible today because it is true; I am convinced it is the Word of God. I am grateful to my parents and grandparents for my Christian heritage; and what I am about to say is not meant to insult them or denigrate their faith. They taught me to believe and live by everything the Bible says. Therefore, as I read the Bible as a child and teenager, I began to ask questions: "Why isn't our Church like the New Testament Church? Why can't we speak in tongues? Why don't we pray for people to be healed? Why are our Church services led by one person and are boring, when in the New Testament Church everybody played a part and they used the gifts of the Spirit? Why do we get rid of our minister when we no longer like him, or he when tells us what we don't want to hear and he tries to change things? Why is the Church run by just a few people? Why do we define ourselves by a label that isn't in the Bible, instead of just calling ourselves Christians?"

As you can imagine, I sometimes got into trouble for asking such questions. I admit I may not always have asked with wisdom and grace; nevertheless, I was gripped by what I had seen of the Church in the Bible. I did not realise at the time that God had shown me something, that I had seen some aspects of restoration, even though I did not use that term in those days. I knew that in the Bible I had seen a Church worthy of the name of Jesus. I just had not yet seen any evidence of it in practice. There was nothing in my immediate frame of reference as a Christian which confirmed that what I had seen actually existed today. However, I could not settle for anything less. I determined as a young man that I would never accept any status quo that was less than what I had seen. (What I saw then has increased in understanding and revelation considerably, and still continues to do so. I still have that single-minded determination today). I am content with my life and can gladly say that I am blessed. I have a wonderful life. However, I can never become complacent. There is always a constant dissatisfaction in me that drives me on, because the status quo of God's restored Church still stands before me. We are not there yet.

A long way to go

The New Testament Church is not the status quo that the Elijah People seek; the restored Church is. That means many things still have to change. The Church has still to grow to maturity and become what it has never yet been. Change is inevitably necessary. The word *repent* literally means to change one's mind. When we become Christians we repent of our sins and everything changes, but there is always constant repentance – change – in our lives if we live from God's status quo. Someone once said that constant change is here to stay. That does not mean we are fickle or that we discard and abandon what we believe, constantly chopping and changing our beliefs, structures and practices to follow the latest fads or Christian fashions. The Elijah People are covenant people, Kingdom people, holy and righteous people. We do not abandon what we believe; we are not like those who are *blown here and there by every wind of teaching and by the cunning and craftiness of men in their deceitful scheming* (Ephesians 4:14).

Neither do the Elijah People hold on with gritted teeth to what they have and refuse to accept there is more, much more. We do not get confined and trapped in our revelation and consequently become more concerned with our own established traditions, reputations and comforts, than God's status quo. God's status quo demands that we continue to develop and grow, and this always necessitates change on our part. I have been shocked to hear people even proudly boast that they belong to a Restoration Church, as if they have arrived at the pinnacle of God's purpose. We do not belong to a Restoration Church; no such Church exists. We belong to the Church that is being restored.

The path to mature sonship demands and necessitates change. The Elijah People are not those who want business as usual or an untroubled, uneventful life. Our leaders are not controlled by programmes and projects, but are captured and motivated by what they have seen of God's ultimate intention for the Church. We are not maintainers of the half-dead but builders of God's restored house. The Elijah People, therefore, must always be brave enough to ask questions, to challenge and confront. We must be like this even with our Church leaders. The Elijah People are obedient, but they are not mute and blindly compliant. The Bible teaches headship, rule and authority; we rightly honour our leaders and submit to them, as the Bible teaches. That does not mean, however, that we cannot ask them questions and even challenge and confront them if we believe that the Church is beginning to settle down and lose its edge. There is a massive difference between asking questions and having a questioning attitude that seeks to undermine or rebel. Godly leaders welcome enquiring and perceptive questions and challenges from their people concerning where the Church stands in the light of God's status quo. If nothing else, it helps keep them focused on the right things. As a prophetic people in the line of Elijah and John the Baptist we also have to be prophetic with ourselves.

Let me assert that this is not a license for the awkward squad to rise up: "I've been waiting to have a go at my leaders; I've got some juicy questions for them!" If you are living under the Lordship of Jesus, your questions, challenges, provocations and confrontations to your leaders and fellow believers will only be because you have seen something of Jesus and his glory. You will be consumed by and concerned with what matters to Jesus, not your own unspiritual, self-motivated and self-promoting agenda. The Gospel will cause its own offence; it doesn't need you to be rude and deliberately offensive in your attitudes. Furthermore, you must also be prepared for your leaders and fellow Elijah People to challenge, provoke and confront you, so that you do not settle for less than God's status quo in your own life. If you are part of the Elijah People you will have friends and leaders to whom you also are accountable.

True faith versus empty religion

Ahab called Elijah a 'bringer of trouble' (1Kings 18:17-18). The second Elijah, John the Baptist, also constantly upset the religious and social apple cart (Luke 3:19-20). He caused havoc among the religious leaders with his radical message of repentance and practical righteousness. He railed against lukewarm religiosity; and when those same proud, self-righteous religious leaders arrived on the scene to inspect him he turned on them:

> *"You brood of snakes!" he exclaimed. "Who warned you to flee God's coming wrath? Prove by the way you live that you have repented of your sins and turned to God. Don't just say to each other, 'We're safe, for we are descendants of Abraham.' That means nothing, for I tell you, God can create children of Abraham from these very stones. Even now the axe of God's judgement is poised, ready to sever the roots of the trees. Yes, every tree that does not produce good fruit will be chopped down and thrown into the fire." (Matthew 3:7-10)*

The Elijah People have no interest in maintaining the status quo of empty religion or the traditions of men in the guise of true faith. They expose it for what it is – a sham. They are inevitably like this because by nature they rattle the cage of the religious status quo. They are told: "just leave things alone; don't rock the boat; be tolerant; don't cause offence; don't be so exclusive; why are you so radical? You mustn't take the Bible so literally. You're too dogmatic." Sometimes our Church is asked to be involved in evangelistic events by certain groups of Christians. They say to me, "You're known as radical people. If you get involved in this project we would prefer it if you didn't insist that new converts need to be baptised in water and speak in tongues. That might upset some of the other Christians." Or they ask us to tone down the radical message of the Gospel of the Kingdom a little: "whatever you do, please don't offend anybody!" My issue with this is that these Christians are never willing to become *more* radical, but always want to promote the importance of compromise, tolerance and moderation. They seek to find the lowest common denominator and appeal to their idea of Church unity to justify their stance. I do not seek to criticise or judge these genuinely good people, but that is not what the Elijah People are concerned with. The Elijah People do not compromise the status quo of God. It sometimes makes them misunderstood and unpopular with other Christians. So be it. We fear God not man. Jim Elliot was incredibly perceptive when he observed:

> *We are so utterly ordinary, so commonplace, while we profess to know a Power the [world] does not reckon with. But we are 'harmless', and therefore unharmed. We are spiritual pacifists, non-militants, conscientious objectors in this battle-to-the-death with principalities and powers in high places. Meekness must be had for contact with men, but brass, outspoken boldness is required to take part in the comradeship of the Cross. We are 'sideliners' – coaching and criticising the real wrestlers while content to sit by and leave the enemies of God unchallenged. The world cannot hate us, we are too much like its own. Oh that God would make us dangerous!*

Holy disturbers

Recently I was told by some members of our Church that some College students new to our city were reluctant to join our Church because we have a reputation for being a Church of radical zealots where it is impossible to hide! I was appalled: what kind of

Christian wants to live anonymously? More seriously: what kind of Church leader is producing such a generation of young men and women who are already running for cover and ready to compromise their passion for Jesus? Aristotle was right when he said: "The only way to avoid criticism is to do nothing, say nothing and be nothing." He could have been describing the condition of many so-called followers of the most radical Person who ever walked this earth, and who walks it today in the Person of his Holy Spirit. I appreciate what Arthur Wallis wrote: "There are too many [traditional, religious] status quos around that need disturbing. Every move of the Holy Spirit is a move of the Holy Disturber."

When Jesus was on earth he was the Holy Disturber; he was definitely a confrontationalist. His strongest opposition during his earthly ministry did not come from the political powers or ordinary people; it came from the national religious status quo, from those who claimed to represent God. The Pharisees, teachers of the Law and the elders of the people constantly attacked him, questioning his identity and motives at every opportunity. They tried to trick him and trip him up with obscure religious questions and sly, underhand actions. They thought themselves superior to Jesus and denied his claims and his authority. Jesus had no time for them; in fact, he went out of his way to expose and offend them. He deliberately did things he knew would upset them: healing people on the Sabbath; claiming to be Yahweh; asking them questions that would trap them in their bigotry. He called them hypocrites (Matthew 23:13) and children of the devil (John 8:44). He deliberately provoked those religious people who hated him; he purposely acted in ways that he knew would enrage them. The notion of a harmless, innocuous Jesus has no basis in the Bible. He made incredible demands on people: he told them that if they wanted to be his disciples they had to eat his flesh and drink his blood (John 6:53-56). We understand what he meant by that, but his immediate hearers were faced with an amazing choice that he did not explain further. Jesus provoked them: 'Take it or leave it: this is what it costs to follow me'. Perhaps the most graphic demonstration of Jesus' confrontation with empty religion occurred when he cleansed the Temple:

> In the temple courts he found men selling cattle, sheep and doves, and others sitting at tables exchanging money. So he made a whip out of cords, and drove all from the temple area, both sheep and cattle; he scattered the coins of the money changers and overturned their tables. To those who sold doves he said, "Get these out of here! How dare you turn my Father's house into a market!" His disciples remembered that it is written: "Zeal for your house will consume me." (John 2:14-17)

Why did Jesus act like this? Religious tradition had replaced God's intention for the Temple: it was meant to be a house of prayer and worship for all the nations. This was where all people, not only Jews, could come and worship God. Tragically, it had become a religious enclave for Jews alone and, to all intents and purposes, nothing more than a commercial enterprise. The priests and other religious leaders had allowed it to degenerate into a narrow, religious and business activity where more attention was given to the mechanics of religion (they needed the animals so they could sacrifice them) than the exercise of true faith and worship. So Jesus cleaned it out. He had no consideration or concern for the reputation of the religious authorities or the property of the traders. He did not whip the people; he used the whip to drive out the animals. He forcefully overturned the money tables, caring nothing for the sensibilities of the dealers. This was God's house and God's status quo had to be restored. Arthur Wallis again: "Like all radicals, Jesus was wholly intolerant of unreality and hypocrisy."

Notice the reason John gave for Jesus' actions: zeal for God's house consumed him (John 2:17). That word *consumed* means to be eaten up. Something ate Jesus up: zeal for his Father's house. Zeal is a dirty word today; it is used to describe those who are so zealous for a cause they are willing to kill themselves and others to achieve their evil ends. Of course, zeal for God's house, God's status quo, God's ultimate intention, cannot entail hatred, murder and suicide bombs. We shall see later that the motivation of the Elijah People is to turn the hearts of people to God out of love for them. The word *zeal* comes from a term meaning to burn in the face; it is what happens to our faces when we get excited – they burn. That is why we often go red or flushed when we get excited. Zeal describes what excites us, what we are passionate about. Jesus was passionate about his Father's status quo.

The Elijah People are passionately concerned with true faith, not empty religion. I am talking here about empty religion that masquerades as Christianity; whatever else it is, it is certainly not genuine Christianity. There are so called Church leaders in my nation who are called on by the media to speak on behalf of God and the Church. They have nothing to say on God's behalf. No national religious institution in which a substantial number of its leaders deny the deity and physical resurrection of Jesus, or a so-called Church that conceals the horrific sexual and physical abuse of children by its priests has any right to speak on behalf of God and the Elijah People. Neither does an independent, unaccountable televangelist speak for the Elijah People. Nor does a charlatan who sells 'prophecies' to susceptible people in the name of Jesus. I actually saw this on television just the other day: a 'preacher' peddling the Gospel of Jesus for money by promising personal prophecies at a price. I saw another selling prayer cloths that guaranteed healing. The various 'God' channels on television are full of slick operators in sharp suits, selling their own brand of 'Christianity' to trusting and genuinely needy viewers. All done in the name of Jesus. How can a 'Church' that denies the uniqueness and authority of the Bible as the Word of God speak for God? How can leaders who parade their own pet theories about heaven and hell, disregarding the eternal truth of Scripture, expect to represent God? How can self-appointed Bible teachers who distort the nature of God to appease those who financially support their ministry be taken seriously? We are the Elijah People, the people of Jesus. Who speaks for God? We do. It's time for the Elijah People to become zealous for God's status quo.

All things are possible

To live according to God's status quo demands faith. Elijah was a man of faith; so are the Elijah People. Faith has four basic elements: hearing God speak; believing what God speaks; confessing what God speaks; and acting on what God speaks:

Faith comes by hearing and hearing by the word of God. (Romans 10:17)

If you confess with your mouth, 'Jesus is Lord,' and believe in your heart that God raised him from the dead, you will be saved. (Romans 10:9)

It is written: 'I believed; therefore I have spoken.' With that same spirit of faith we also believe and therefore speak. (2Corinthians 4:13)

Do not merely listen to the word and so deceive yourselves. Do what it says. (James 1:22)

Elijah heard God speak to him. 1Kings 17:1 tells us that he stood in the presence of Yahweh; he was perfectly placed to hear the voice of God. God spoke to Elijah; he told him there would be no rain for a long time. Elijah heard that word and believed it. Then he spoke it out; he agreed with and confessed it. The word *confess* means to say the same as; to speak agreement with something somebody said. Then Elijah acted on what he had heard, believed and confessed.

We see many instances of Elijah's faith in action. This very first act before Ahab demanded that Elijah exercise his faith. Elijah spoke something into being that did not yet exist; but he exercised his faith. Then he heard God tell him to leave where he was and that God would look after him by ordering ravens to feed him (1Kings 17:4). Elijah had just prophesied to Israel that there would be no rain until he said so. That meant no harvest, no food. God said to him, "I will look after you in all this. I will feed you. I will send ravens twice a day with breakfast and dinner. They will bring you bread and meat." Anybody who knows anything about ravens knows one thing: they love meat. What an apparently crazy thing for God to do: to provide meat for his servant via a bird that loves carrion, that eats anything, especially meat. To the natural mind, this sounds like one of God's less clever ideas. Nevertheless, the ravens came, just like God said they would, and fed Elijah with fresh meat.

Elijah exercised his faith at Zarephath. His word of faith released a constant supply of flour and oil for the widow (1Kings 17:14-16). Then came the great miracle of raising the widow's son from the dead. Elijah was the first person in the Bible to raise somebody from the dead. He had no reference point for what he did, except that he knew the living God, the Author of life. Elijah knew that death was contrary to God's nature and his intention for humanity. He knew that the living God is the God of life and the God of restoration. Elijah was incensed by the injustice of the widow's loss of her son; she had been robbed by the devil. So Elijah exercised his faith in the God of the living by raising the young man from death and restored him to his mother. Faith refuses to accept any status quo that is contrary to God's will and purpose.

After this came the great showdown with the prophets of Baal-Melqart, when Elijah called down the fire from heaven. In each of these instances of faith and all the others in Elijah's life we see how he established God's status quo in every situation by acts of faith. He heard what God wanted, believed it, spoke it and then brought it into being. Elijah constantly challenged people to have faith; his own faith was a prophetic example to them. He refused to allow the status quo of unbelief, with its accompanying mediocrity, compromise and refusal to change, dominate his life and that of the people. He established God's status quo through his faith, living by the simple maxim: God said it; I believe it; that settles it.

The Elijah People are faith people. It takes faith to see the restoration of all things. It takes faith to see the restored Church, worthy of Jesus. It takes faith to see the earth filled with the knowledge of the glory of the Lord as the waters cover the sea (Habakkuk 2:14). It takes faith to see the Bride of Christ who has made herself ready for her Bridegroom (Revelation 19:7; 21:2). It takes faith to see the sons of God coming to maturity. It takes faith to live as a Christian.

After the victory at Mount Carmel, Elijah continued to move in faith by praying: *Elijah climbed to the top of Carmel, bent down to the ground and put his face between his knees* (1Kings 18:42). That was a particularly strange and uncomfortable thing to do. He bent low to the ground and put his face between his knees. Why did Elijah pray like that? In doing this, his physical ears would not hear anything that would adversely affect his faith. In his spirit Elijah had already heard the sound of rain. For him it was already raining; by faith he could hear the sound. It was as real as the sound of actual rain. It just had not physically manifested yet. Elijah wanted to shut out any obstacle or distraction that would prevent his faith being actualised. Furthermore, to the natural person, Elijah looked ridiculous: a grown man in full view of everybody, with his face between his knees. Elijah cared nothing for his own personal reputation. He did not concern himself with what others thought about him. When you begin to put God first and live by faith in him you have to kiss your reputation goodbye. God is more concerned with his glory than your comfort and reputation. To the unspiritual, unbelieving person, faith is ridiculous. To the spiritual person, faith is the most natural thing in the universe. We are designed by God to live by faith; it is easy to live by faith. The Bible says: *Without faith it is impossible to please God* (Hebrews 11:6).

Some think that it is so hard to please God because faith is so hard. That is completely wrong. It is easy to please God: all you have to do is have faith in him. Because God is good and because he knows we need faith, he graciously gives it to us. He enables us to have the faith to believe him:

It is by grace you have been saved, through faith – and this not from yourselves – it is the gift of God. (Ephesians 2:8)

To the natural, unspiritual, religious, unbelieving person, the notion of God's status quo and the restoration of all things is either nonsense or a pipe dream. To the Elijah People, the people of faith, it is happening right now. We hear its sound and we see it with our eyes. The restoration of all things is happening right in front of us; in fact, it is happening through us. Do you perceive it?

SEVEN

Status Quo (2)

The word of Yahweh came to Elijah. (1Kings 18:1)

The word of God came to John. (Luke 3:2)

The Word of the Lord

God establishes his status quo through his word, and his word establishes his will. God's will is his status quo. Every act of creation in Genesis was preceded by God speaking: 'Let there be.' Jesus is the Word of God (John 1:1); he is God's ultimate communication and revelation of himself to us. Elijah was a prophet of God: as such he heard God speak and then spoke what God told him to say. That is the essence of prophecy. However, Elijah was more than somebody who merely heard from God and spoke: for a while he was *the* voice of God to his world. Several times during his story we find the phrase, 'the word of the LORD [Yahweh] came to Elijah' (1Kings 17:2,8; 18:1; 19:9). Elijah was the prophetic voice of God to his world so that people could hear clearly what God said and respond accordingly. He spoke plainly:

"As Yahweh, the God of Israel lives, there will be neither dew nor rain in the next few years except at my word." (1Kings 17:1)

"The god who answers by fire – he is God."
(1Kings 18:24)

Each time the word of God came to Elijah, it also marked a determining point in his own life, directing him, correcting and encouraging him, and maturing him. Elijah lived by the prophetic word of God that came to him, and by the words that God had spoken to previous generations through those like Abraham, Moses, Joshua and David. It established God's status quo in his life. Consequently, his word was powerful and authoritative: he said it would not rain and it didn't. He prayed to God over the body of the dead boy and the boy was raised to life. He called down fire from heaven and it fell. He accurately foretold the way in which Ahab and Jezebel would die. He told king Ahaziah he would not recover from his sickness:

"You will never leave the bed you are lying on.
You will certainly die!" So Ahaziah died, according
to the word of Yahweh that Elijah had spoken.
(2Kings 1:16-17)

Elijah understood that, as a prophet, first of all he had the privilege and the responsibility of hearing God speak. He believed God was a God who spoke, who always had something to say, and who expected to be heard and obeyed. Elijah knew that his priority in life was to be a man who heard from God. Then, out from that place of hearing, he also had the equally valuable privilege and responsibility of speaking the word of God that he had heard. The word of the Lord came to Elijah only because he took the time to hear it, and then he had to obey God by speaking what he had heard. An important facet of Elijah's prophetic ministry was his ability to discern the voice of God amidst everything else that was going on around him. This was powerfully demonstrated when Elijah fled from Jezebel and hid in the cave. Despite the intense personal pressure he was going through, he was still able to hear the voice of God:

Yahweh said, "Go out and stand on the mountain in the presence of Yahweh, for Yahweh is about to pass by." Then a great and powerful wind tore the mountains apart and shattered the rocks before Yahweh, but Yahweh was not in the wind. After the wind there was an earthquake, but Yahweh was not in the earthquake. After the earthquake came a fire, but Yahweh was not in the fire. And after the fire came a gentle whisper. When Elijah heard it, he pulled his cloak over his face and went out and stood at the mouth of the cave. Then a voice said to him, "What are you doing here, Elijah?" (1Kings 19:11-13)

As we shall see later, the wind and fire are often symbolic of the Holy Spirit. However, Elijah was so used to hearing God's voice, he did not automatically assume that Yahweh was speaking to him through these phenomena. He had learned not to depend on his natural senses when relating to God; he had trained himself to hear the most important voice that any person can hear. On this occasion it was not a loud, booming shout, but a gentle whisper, or as the older versions of the Bible say: a still, small voice.

John the Baptist, too, was a man of the word of God. He began his ministry only when the word of God came to him (Luke 3:2). He had been living in the wilderness for a long time, perhaps years, before he began his ministry. During that time he had waited upon God in preparation for what God would do through him. It is interesting that the first word of God that came from John's lips when he began his public ministry was a quotation from the written Word of God, the Old Testament, from the prophet Isaiah:

> *A voice of one calling in the desert, 'Prepare the way for the Lord, make straight paths for him. Every valley shall be filled in, every mountain and hill made low. The crooked roads shall become straight, the rough ways smooth. And all mankind will see God's salvation.' (Luke 3:4-6, citing Isaiah 40:3-5)*

The Elijah People are people of the Word of God. First of all they are people of the Book of God: the Bible. God establishes his status quo through his Word; the Bible is the spoken word of God written down. We believe in its integrity and reliability; we live under its authority. I do not have space in this book to present a detailed doctrine of the Bible; but I do need to say a few basic things about it:

First, the Bible is 'God breathed' (2Timothy 3:16). Older versions have *inspired*, but 'God breathed' is more accurate. The word here literally means 'breathed out by God'. The Bible is not a human book about God; it is a book written by God himself. It came from within God's own being; he breathed it out, communicating his word to the human authors.

Second, it is *inerrant*: it has no errors or contradictions: 'As for God, his way is perfect; the word of Yahweh is flawless' (2Samuel 22:31). It tells us the truth about God and ourselves. It records history one hundred percent accurately. It is eternally correct and accurate in what it says about issues such as marriage and sexuality: that marriage is between a man and woman; that homosexuality is sinful. It is not a book confined to or defined by the cultures it was written in; it is the eternal, unchanging Book of God for every generation. If you interpret and define the Bible through any culture, then when that culture changes your interpretation of the Bible necessarily has to change. You must interpret culture through the Bible.

Third, it is *infallible*: it does not deceive us but leads us into all truth: 'Your word is a lamp to my feet and a light for my path' (Psalm 119:105). It never leads us into confusion or plays tricks with us. It never takes us up dead end streets or down blind alleys. It has to be handled correctly and treated properly. It must be interpreted in the right way. Each part must be read in the light of the whole; and the whole is the sum of all its parts.

Jesus and the Bible

Jesus is greater than the Bible. He is the God who created the world and who, together with the Father and the Spirit, breathed out the Word of God from within him. Yet while he was here on earth he never usurped the authority of the Word of God by imposing on it his own authority as God. In fact, he fully submitted to its authority in his life and ministry. That is why you will often find an incident in his life followed by the phrase, 'this happened to fulfil the word of the prophet' or 'these things happened so that the scripture might be fulfilled'.

(The Gospels are full of instances like this). Let me mention two in particular; they are fascinating because they are Old Testament prophecies that were fulfilled at Jesus' crucifixion, when Jesus was, if you like, powerless to control the situation.

> *When the soldiers crucified Jesus, they took his clothes, dividing them into four shares, one for each of them, with the undergarment remaining. This garment was seamless, woven in one piece from top to bottom. "Let's not tear it," they said to one another. "Let's decide by lot who will get it." This happened that the scripture might be fulfilled which said, "They divided my garments among them and cast lots for my clothing." So this is what the soldiers did. (John 19:23-24)*

> *When they came to Jesus and found that he was already dead, they did not break his legs. Instead, one of the soldiers pierced Jesus' side with a spear, bringing a sudden flow of blood and water. The man who saw it has given testimony, and his testimony is true. He knows that he tells the truth, and he testifies so that you also may believe. These things happened so that the scripture would be fulfilled: "Not one of his bones will be broken," and, as another scripture says, "They will look on the one they have pierced." (John 19:33-37)*

Both these Scriptures demonstrate the divine power and authority of the Word of God. Jesus could not determine or direct what was happening to him at the time: he was helpless. The soldiers had no idea that their actions were fulfilling Scripture: they were Romans who probably had little or no knowledge of the Word of God. Nevertheless, because the Bible has such integrity, power and authority, its self-fulfilment occurred even here.

What does this mean practically for the Elijah People? Simply, that we allow the Bible to be the decider and determiner of our lives. We not only believe it to be the Word of God: we live by it and do what it says. Francis Chan put it well: "I want my life to fit in this book." Today it is popular, even among so-called Christian leaders, to diminish the Word of God and erode its teachings on subjects such as hell, marriage, sexuality, the uniqueness of Jesus, money, and the end times – to name just a few. They take liberties with God's Word written down, twisting it and making it say what they want it to say. They assert it cannot be uniquely authoritative and relevant to twenty-first century humanity. But what is so special about the twenty-first century? The needs and sinful condition of humanity have not changed since Adam disobeyed. Sin is sin, whatever century or culture we live in. The Gospel of the Kingdom is eternal; it does not compromise itself to suit a decade or a culture. Church leaders who question and erode the authority of the Bible wonder why their Churches are emptying and the lives of their people have no solid basis. They look quizzically and with a little superiority at Churches that continue to assert the authority of the Bible and which grow at a tremendous rate, failing to acknowledge that there is a correlation between these two aspects. Jesus is Lord where his Word is supreme, not merely in theory, but in practice. Any Church that puts its traditions on a par with or even above the Bible ceases to be the Church.

To be counted radical today all you have to do is believe the whole Bible and live according to it. Take a simple yet very important teaching in the Bible: disciplining children. The Bible is very clear about physical discipline: it must be administered at the right time in the right way:

Folly is bound up in the heart of a child, but the rod of discipline will drive it far from him. (Proverbs 22:15)

Do not withhold discipline from a child; if you punish him with the rod, he will not die. (Proverbs 23:13)

The rod of correction imparts wisdom, but a child left to himself disgraces his mother. (Proverbs 29:15)

There it is in black and white. When necessary, my father disciplined me with physical punishment; I did the same for my children. The Bible says it must be done at the right time and in the correct manner. My dad did not beat me: he inflicted pain with his slipper on the place God has specifically designed for the purpose – the backside! This flies in the face of some modern thinkers, even Christians, who accuse us of beating our children, abusing them and infringing their human rights. In some countries it is even illegal to smack or spank a child. Our schools, families, Churches and societies are paying the price for ignoring and departing from the Word of God. Of course, along with every right-minded person, I utterly condemn child abuse in every form it takes.

Anybody who mistreats children physically, mentally or sexually is unimaginably evil. But that is not what the biblical discipline of a child is all about. This might seem a trivial matter, but it is what the Bible teaches. Therefore, it is not trivial, but of fundamental, eternal importance in the matter of raising children.

Defend your lentil fields

Tony Ling preaches a powerful message about a man called Shammah who defended a lentil field against the Philistines:

> *When the Philistines banded together at a place where there was a field full of lentils, Israel's troops fled from them. But Shammah took his stand in the middle of the field. He defended it and struck the Philistines down, and Yahweh brought about a great victory. (2Samuel 23:11-12)*

Tony asks: why did Shammah take his stand and fight to protect a lentil field? It was not particularly strategic or important; it was only a field full of lentils. Nevertheless, Shammah knew that the Philistines would not stop there: if they defeated him in the lentil field they would continue to push him back in retreat. He would soon have to defend and fight for much more important places. He would have to take his stand somewhere; otherwise he would eventually lose everything.

The Elijah People do not compromise on the Word of God: we take our stand in our 'lentil fields'. We resist the pressure to compromise the integrity and ultimate authority of the Bible or forsake its eternal truth. We reject the pressure to be more tolerant and give way on the truth of the eternal Word of God. Rather, we release its power into our lives by submitting to its authority and power in every area of life. We are not concerned merely with doctrinal truth and purity, even though that is very important. The Word of God is powerful; it is living and active (Hebrews 4:12). We are a people who put it into practice and build our lives on it. For example, we bring God what belongs to him in the tithe and give him freewill offerings because it teaches us to; therefore we are blessed and empowered to bless others. We lay hands on sick people in the name of Jesus and they recover. We forgive those who sin against us and are reconciled to them. We are baptised in the Holy Spirit and speak in tongues, releasing all the Divine ability of the indwelling Holy Spirit. We believe in a God of the impossible and we see him do the impossible! Christopher Wright beautifully encapsulates the centrality and controlling dimension of the Bible for the Elijah People:

> We talk about the problems of 'applying the Bible to our lives', which often means modifying the Bible somewhat adjectivally to fit into the assumed 'reality' of the life we live 'in the real world'. What would it mean to apply our lives to the Bible instead, assuming the Bible to be the reality - the real story - to which we are called to conform ourselves?

God has spoken

We have made the point that both Elijah and John the Baptist were prophets: they heard God speak to them and then they spoke that word to their world. Elijah's actual, spoken words had power to shut up the sky, and to call fire from heaven. He and John spoke with relevance and clarity so that their hearers were left in no doubt what God was speaking to them. John the Baptist was intensely practical in what he told those who came to see him: "Give one of your two shirts to the poor; don't collect more taxes than the government requires; don't extort money; be content with your pay; don't accuse people falsely" (see Luke 3:10-14). The Elijah People also speak the Word of the Lord. We do not only believe in, and live by, the Bible: we speak out what the Bible says and what God speaks to each particular generation and culture. A.W. Tozer said: "The Bible sends us out into the world but never to compromise with or walk in the way of the world." Therefore, we address the issues of our day and time to the Church and the world. The Elijah People are a prophetic people, and prophets speak for God as his representatives and his voice.

I am acutely aware that I am writing at a unique time in God's restoration purpose. The time and culture I live in has its own hallmarks and its own particular issues that the Elijah People must speak about. Each Elijah People generation has its own issues to face and to bring to the attention of the world. Francis Schaeffer said: "The Christian must resist the spirit of the world in the form it takes in his own generation." God is always speaking from his status quo to the religious and spiritual, to the political and social, and to the moral arenas in which we find ourselves. He speaks through his prophets – the Elijah People. In order not to become outdated, I do not intend to itemise each of the issues that my Elijah People generation must currently address; they also vary from nation to nation, from decade to decade, from culture to culture, and from time to time. The important thing is that we keep God's plan and purpose and the Word of God as our status quo. Then each issue that rises up against that status quo or attempts to nullify it is swiftly exposed for what it really is. I should like to suggest that there are three kinds of prophetic words that the Elijah People speak in order to establish God's status quo.

1. Words of Judgement

Confrontation: Elijah and John the Baptist spoke prophetic words of judgement. First of all, their words were words of confrontation. As already mentioned, Elijah confronted Ahab and Jezebel concerning specific issues: false religion; the murder of Naboth. He confronted the prophets of Baal-Melqart, challenging and denying the very existence of their god and proving the truth of his word through signs and wonders. John the Baptist confronted the Pharisees, calling them a brood of snakes. (Jesus did the same in Matthew 23:33). He confronted Herod concerning Herod's unlawful marriage and his immorality. He even confronted the ungodly behaviour of the occupying Roman military. Elijah and John were not afraid to use the words *sin, wrong* and *repent*. We might say they were black and white in their accurate assessments of situations and the spiritual condition of their hearers. To use a modern idiom: they called a spade a spade.

Confrontation is an inevitable and necessary characteristic of the Elijah People. We confront unrighteousness wherever and whenever it raises its demonic head, whether it is in the Church or in society. We speak out against injustice and the accepted norms of our day that contradict the Word and will of God: moral and ethical issues, political and social issues; and religious issues. A.W. Tozer wrote: "We are not diplomats, but prophets, and our message is not a compromise but an ultimatum." In his famous *Letter from a Birmingham Jail*, Martin Luther King wrote:

There was a time when the church was very powerful - in the time when the early Christians rejoiced at being deemed worthy to suffer for what they believed. In those days the church was not merely a thermometer that recorded the ideas and principles of popular opinion; it was a thermostat that transformed the mores of society. Whenever the early Christians entered a town, the people in power became disturbed and immediately sought to convict the Christians for being 'disturbers of the peace' and 'outside agitators.' But the Christians pressed on, in the conviction that they were 'a colony of heaven,' called to obey God rather than man. Small in number, they were big in commitment. They were too God-intoxicated to be 'astronomically intimidated'. Things are different now. So often the contemporary church is a weak, ineffectual voice with an uncertain sound. So often it is an arch-defender of the status quo. Far from being disturbed by the presence of the church, the power structure of the average community is consoled by the church's silent - and often even vocal - sanction of things as they are.

The Elijah People refuse to accept society's warm embrace of unbiblical moral values, the destruction of marriage, the compromises of religious leaders on biblical truth, the extortion of the poor, racial prejudice and hatred, the erosion of biblical, family values, the notion of a Christianity that is insipid and irrelevant which the media persist in conveying. To stand for God means we stand against the world and the values that the world attempts to impose on the Church through spiritual blackmail, coercion, political pressure and unrighteous legislation. We stand against and confront the Church when it sells out to the world. The author and theologian William Inge is reputed to have said: "The Church that is married to the spirit of this age will be a widow in the next." We use all means and avenues available to speak this word of prophetic ultimatum: the modern world has made it easy for any voice to be heard, including God's.

Some of the Elijah People will enter the worlds of politics and social activism; others the arenas of business and health care; still others the spheres of education, the media and arts. There is also the world of writing and the world of video. The speed and easy availability of the internet and social media mean that words and images fly around the globe in seconds via computers and modern mobile or cell phones, resulting in the speedy overthrow of unrighteous despotic governments and corrupt political systems. And don't forget the power of the preaching of the Word of God. There remains a place for the man or woman of God to stand up each week and bring the Word of the Lord to hundreds and thousands, even millions, of hearers. The Elijah People are a prophetic irritant to humanity's status quo, to anything that is contrary to God's restoration purpose, and must utilise every righteous tool that is available to establish God's status quo.

Commendation: While the Elijah People are confrontational in their prophetic words of judgement, they are also quick to speak words of commendation. Far too many Christians are swift in their negative criticisms but fail to bless and commend when necessary. (Even words of confrontation are spoken to change things for the better). It is the responsibility of the Elijah People also to commend wherever and whenever righteousness prevails; when governments pass laws that are in line with the laws of God; when honesty, truth, and respect are promoted and honoured; when the Church walks in the truth and beauty of holiness; when right things are done, even by unrighteous people. Some years ago I agreed to marry a couple who were not Christians, and who had no interest whatsoever in Jesus. The bride was the daughter of my friends and she asked me if I would perform her marriage ceremony. I gladly agreed to do so. However, I was quizzed by some Christians, who questioned how I as a Christian could marry two people who had no faith in Jesus. My answer was simple: God honours all marriages, not only Christian marriages. God instituted marriage, and even though this couple did not believe in Jesus, nevertheless, the fact that they were doing what God instituted in his Word for all couples meant that God would honour their act. God is for marriage, not only Christian marriage. God loves families, not merely Christian families. God loves people, not only Christians. The Elijah People, therefore, should be consistent in our confrontation and in our commendation. In doing so we convey to our world that God is consistent: he loves righteousness and hates lawlessness (Hebrews 1:8-9). Thus his judgements are always right and true.

2. Words of Hope

One of the characteristics of people without God is that they have no hope. God sent Elijah to Zarephath for him to be cared for by a widow (1Kings 17). Elijah went there as a bringer of hope. This widow had very little and expected to die soon: in effect, she had lost all hope. Then Elijah arrived. The widow knew who he was; his fame had gone before him. She knew that he was the man whose name was *Yahweh is my God*. Hope had tangibly arrived in the shape of the man whose God was Yahweh. Elijah spoke the word of hope to her:

"The jar of flour will not be used up and the jug of oil will not run dry until the day Yahweh gives rain on the land". (1Kings 17:14)

Elijah gave the widow hope for her future and then delivered on his promise; she did not die. Later, the widow was struck by the most appalling tragedy that can befall a mother: her child died. Even in this dreadful, heart-wrenching situation, Elijah again gave her hope. He said to the widow, "Give me your son" (1Kings 17:19). Imagine her uncontrollable and overwhelming joy when Elijah presented her with her child, newly raised from the dead:

The woman said to Elijah, "Now I know that you are a man of God and that the word of Yahweh from your mouth is the truth." (1Kings 17:24)

Here was an ordinary woman, a widow with a young child, whose non-existent god Baal-Melqart had failed her in every regard, now overjoyed and overwhelmed, because through Elijah the living God provided all that she needed to eat and drink, along with her son – raised from the dead and restored to life and to his mother! Only the God of hope can do that.

The Elijah People are people of hope who give the hope of God to others. We have to differentiate between two kinds of hope: the natural hope of the world and the hope that comes from God. The world's hope, or natural hope, is a hope that wishes for the best but is always tinged to varying degrees with doubt, uncertainty or fear. People hope for the best but fear the worst. They hope their team will win, but know they might not. They hope they will pass the examination or get the job, but fear that they will be unsuccessful. They hope they are lucky, so they cross their fingers and touch wood, or carry out certain rituals like putting on the left sock before the right one, or they avoid leaving their house on Friday the 13th. This is what the world means when it talks about hope.

The kind of hope the Bible talks about is different from worldly hope. Bible hope is the certain, confident, unwavering expectation of good. Bible hope is hope in God. Hope is linked to faith (Hebrews 11:1). Hope is the coat peg of faith; you hang your faith on your hope. In fact, you cannot have faith without hope. Bible hope has no 'perhaps', 'maybe', or 'possibly'. It is a definite, confident expectation of good. Christians do not need luck to live in the hope of God.

Hope in God is to do with the future, both the imminent future and the distant future; for tomorrow and next year. Hope in God tells us that we have a future and a future that is good, because hope's reference point, hope's focus, hope's source, is God – he is the God of hope (Romans 15:13). How are we able to have hope in God? Because God is the God of our future, not only of our past and present. Restoration means there must be a glorious future. God is a good God with good plans for us:

> "I know the plans I have for you," declares Yahweh, "plans to prosper you and not to harm you; plans to give you hope and a future." (Jeremiah 29:11).

We hope in God with a certain, confident expectation that our future will be better than the past and the present; that everything will work out for our good. This is our certain, confident expectation. Hope, therefore, is an important element in restoration. To hope in God is to trust him at all times, in good times and the bad. To hope in God is to trust him for the future; that the future will be good. Even if the future brings hardship and difficulties, our hope in God remains the same; it is not affected or determined by our circumstances. When Daniel's three friends faced the prospect of being thrown into a blazing furnace because of their refusal to worship Nebuchadnezzar, they faced it with their hope in God intact, confidently speaking out that hope:

> Shadrach, Meshach and Abednego replied to the king, "O Nebuchadnezzar, we do not need to defend ourselves before you in this matter. If we are thrown into the blazing furnace, the God we serve is able to save us from it, and he will rescue us from your hand, O king. But even if he does not, we want you to know, O king, that we will

not serve your gods or worship the image of gold you have set up." (Daniel 3:16-18)

We hope in God not only for the ultimate or distant future, but for the immediate future: for the rest of the day, for tomorrow, next week, next year, the years to come. We live in hope every second of our lives And if we die, we die in certain hope of meeting Jesus and of the resurrection to come for all. Hope in God involves having an unshakeable confidence, a certainty and unwavering trust in him. Hope in God is linked to faith, for faith brings the hope of the future into the present. Faith is the 'now' of our future hope. Hope in God means we do not depend on things, circumstances, or situations we can or cannot control for our happiness and well-being. Our well-being does not depend on our circumstances, situations, or material possessions; our hope is in God. Hope, therefore, looks to the future with unshakeable confidence and certainty because God is the same in the future as he is in the present, and as he was in the past. He is unchanging and eternal. So we anticipate what is to come with peace, joy and faith (Romans 15:13), not dread and fear. We overflow with hope!

God is the object of our hope – we hope in him and in his Word – who he is and what he says. Because God has hope for us he has a future for us. Hope looks to the future with confidence and peace. Hope in God defines and determines how we live in the present. As the Elijah People, this is the hope we speak to a hopeless world. Jesus is our hope (1Timothy 1:1); he alone is the hope for everyone, no matter how desperate their situation. Just as Elijah spoke hope and brought hope to the widow and miraculously released a supply of flour and oil, and raised her child from the dead, so the Elijah People are empowered to bring the miraculous, hope-filled, resurrection life of Jesus to those who have no hope:

Let us hold unswervingly to the hope we profess, for he who promised is faithful. (Hebrews 10:23)

3. Words of Creative Power

Elijah's prophetic words were creative and powerful: he brought things into being through his word. Because he lived in the presence of God, he constantly heard God's voice and thus was enabled to speak what he heard before it was manifested on the earth. Elijah's word resulted in a famine and drought that would not cease until he said so. It did not rain for three and a half years because he said so. The rain came when he said it would. The fire fell from heaven as the result of his word. Ahab, Jezebel and Ahaziah all died at the time and in the manner Elijah said they would. Things happened – or did not happen – because Elijah said so. His word was God's word. The key aspect of this dimension of his ministry was that Elijah heard and saw what was to come and spoke it into being.

The Elijah People are not today's people, consumed by and concerned only with what is happening in the immediacy of our circumstances; we are tomorrow's people, the people of the future living in today. We are those who have seen the future, we have tasted of the power of the age to come (Hebrews 6:5). We are those who see what is ahead in the purpose of God and speak it out in faith and hope. We hear what the Spirit is saying to the Church and the world, speak his word to the

Church and the world, and then, as much as lies within us, we manifest that word by living it now. Remember: God always creates by speaking: every act of creation in Genesis was preceded by God's spoken word: "Let there be." King David saw what was ahead and spoke of the resurrection of Jesus (Acts 2:31), one thousand years before the event. Peter called David a prophet (Acts 2:30). The Elijah People see what is ahead and call it into reality. We do not shirk from our calling in this regard, but speak boldly of the restored Church, the spotless Bride, the glorious City, the mature sons of God, and the earth filled with the knowledge of the glory of the Lord as the waters cover the sea (Habakkuk 2:14). These are not unattainable ideals; they already exist in the heart of God and he has spoken them into existence. For the Elijah People they are also real, now in this time. We speak and prophesy of all that the Church is yet to be in God's restoration purpose and plan. Furthermore, we become in reality what we have seen and heard in the presence of God. We are becoming the fulfilment of the Word of the Lord that we speak. We increasingly become what we have seen and so the restoration of all things is worked out through us.

EIGHT

Spirit and Power

*He will go on before the Lord in the spirit
and power of Elijah. (Luke 1:17)*

Elijah was at home in the realm of the supernatural. He was a man who knew the Holy Spirit. While we do not see many specific mentions of the Holy Spirit in the story of Elijah, we certainly do see significant examples of the Spirit's activity in and through him. Signs and wonders of the Spirit regularly accompanied him: fire from heaven, raising the dead, creative miracles, supernatural strength, (he ran twenty miles [32 kilometres] from Carmel to Jezreel in the power of the Spirit), the parting of the river Jordan. When Obadiah met Elijah prior to the encounter on Mount Carmel, he was frightened that Elijah would disappear because the Spirit of the Lord might carry him away (1Kings 18:12). Elijah's environment and lifestyle was the sphere of the Holy Spirit.

Gabriel described John the Baptist as the one who would go on before the Lord 'in the spirit and power of Elijah' (Luke 1:17). John, the second Elijah, was filled with the Holy Spirit when he was still in his mother's womb (Luke 1:16). He grew and became 'strong in the Spirit' (Luke 1:80); and lived every moment of his life filled with the Holy Spirit. To be like Elijah, to have that Elijah type of ministry, John the Baptist had to be a man filled with God the Holy Spirit.

Fire and Wind

The Holy Spirit does not have a body. He cannot be seen, so the Bible uses different images to describe him more clearly and to explain some of the things he does when he manifests himself. Helpfully these are everyday, familiar images, which make it easier for us to understand the Spirit. When we read the story of Elijah it is evident that fire played a significant role in his life and prophetic function. He called down fire from heaven in the encounter at Carmel; when Ahaziah sent soldiers to arrest him, fire fell from heaven twice to confirm he was a man of God (2Kings 1:10-12). Finally, when Elijah went to heaven:

Suddenly, a chariot of fire and horses of fire appeared and separated Elijah and Elisha, and Elijah went up to heaven in a whirlwind. (2Kings 2:11)

It is no coincidence that John the Baptist declared that Jesus would baptise his Elijah People 'in the Holy Spirit and fire' (Matthew 3:11). Of course, we know that on the Day of Pentecost, when the Holy Spirit was sent from heaven to empower the Elijah People, he came as fire:

They saw what seemed to be tongues of fire that separated and came to rest on each of them. All of them were filled with the Holy Spirit and began to speak in other languages as the Spirit enabled them. (Acts 2:3-4)

God is a consuming fire (Hebrews 12:29). In the Old Testament God regularly revealed himself in fire. He met Moses in a burning bush (Exodus 3:1-4); a pillar of cloud and fire accompanied the Israelites for forty years in the desert (Exodus 40:36-38); God judged sin with fire (Leviticus 10:1-3; Numbers 11:1-3). The image of the Holy Spirit as fire in the Bible indicates the presence of God; holiness and judgement; and zeal (remember, we said that zeal means to burn in the face). Paul urged the Thessalonian Church: *Do not put out the Spirit's fire* (1Thessalonians 5:19).

Perhaps the most significant moment of Elijah's earthly life was the moment he left to go to heaven: he ascended in a whirlwind. Elijah went to heaven in a Holy Spirit hurricane! The wind is another major biblical image used to describe the Holy Spirit. The Hebrew word for Spirit (*ruach*) and the Greek word (*pneuma*) both literally mean 'wind' or 'breath'. In the Old Testament probably the most well known example where the wind and breath are used to describe the Spirit of God is found in Ezekiel chapter 37. And at Pentecost, before the one hundred twenty believers saw the tongues of fire: *A sound like the blowing of a violent wind came from heaven and filled the whole house where they were sitting* (Acts 2:2).

The image of the Holy Spirit as the wind reminds us that he is invisible and can only be known by faith; that he is continually on the move (wind is air in motion); that even though we cannot see him we can feel him and see his effects; that he is powerful and cannot be controlled by us; and that he blows with varying degrees – from the gentle breeze to the violent hurricane. In the same way that humans cannot live without breathing, so the Holy Spirit is vital and necessary for our spiritual life.

These images of the Holy Spirit as fire and the wind powerfully demonstrate to us that Elijah was undoubtedly a man of the Spirit. That is why Gabriel said to Zechariah that John the Baptist would go on before the Lord in the spirit and power of Elijah. John had to be filled with the Spirit to qualify as the second Elijah. As I have already mentioned, John summarised Jesus' forthcoming earthly ministry in terms of the Holy Spirit:

"I baptise you in water for repentance. But after me will come one who is more powerful than I, whose sandals I am not fit to carry. He will baptise you in the Holy Spirit and fire." (Matthew 3:11)

In effect, John stated here that the reason why Jesus had come to earth and live among us was to baptise us in the Holy Spirit. When John made this statement Jesus had not yet been baptised, died on the Cross, risen from the dead or ascended to heaven. Yet, in this particular declaration, John made no mention of these vitally important aspects of Jesus' ministry: in his prophetic foresight he spoke about the Holy Spirit. That tells me the Holy Spirit has a vital, central role to play in the life of the Elijah People. The Spirit raised Jesus from the dead so that Jesus could baptise his Elijah People in the Spirit.

The Preeminent Spirit

The Holy Spirit, therefore, is preeminent in the lives of the Elijah People. That might sound somewhat strange in view of all I have been saying thus far concerning God the Father's purpose for the world: to fill it with a people who are just like his Son, Jesus.

Furthermore, the New Testament itself states that Jesus has the preeminence or supremacy in everything (Colossians 1:18). However, only a preeminent Holy Spirit can establish a preeminent Jesus in the Church. It is the purpose of the Holy Spirit to achieve the preeminence of Jesus and the purpose of the Father, and fill the earth with the Elijah People: the mature sons of God, who are like their Lord and elder brother. This was the whole emphasis of Jesus when he spoke in depth to the disciples about the Holy Spirit. He told them that it was for their good he was going away (John 16:7), because he could send the Spirit only if he went to heaven. As you read these chapters in John you discover that the only way we can know the Father and the Son is through the Spirit. When the Spirit indwells us we also have the Father and the Son within us (he is the Spirit of the Father and the Spirit of the Son). It is of great significance that almost the last thing Jesus spoke to his disciples about before his suffering and death was their forthcoming relationship with him through the Holy Spirit (see John chapters 14 to 16).

When the Holy Spirit came at Pentecost we are told that the fire *came to rest on each of them* (Acts 2:4). That same term is used to describe what Jesus did when he ascended to heaven as King of kings and Lord of lords: *he sat down at the right hand of the Majesty in heaven* (Hebrews 1:3). The Spirit came to enact in the lives of the Church on earth exactly what Jesus was doing in heaven: ruling all things from his throne. The Holy Spirit is the Spirit of the King of the Kingdom; he lives within us, ruling us with the authority and power of our heavenly King. Right now, if you are a believer, Jesus is 'sitting on you' as Lord in the Person of the Holy Spirit. He is enthroned in your life.

Life in the Spirit

When we are born again, we receive the Person of the Holy Spirit in all his fullness. At the moment of new birth, every believer receives the same measure or amount of the Holy Spirit; he is not divided up or portioned out to us depending on our calling, race, age, or gender: *Of his fullness we have all received, and grace upon grace* (John 1:16).

Each one of us who has received Jesus as Lord has the entire Holy Spirit – all of God himself – living in us. Each one of us is filled with the same Person in all his fullness: he who hovered over the waters in the creation; he who raised Jesus from the dead; he who came from heaven at Pentecost. We all have all of the Spirit. And the Spirit lives in us all with the same degree of ability or power: we all have the same ability, the same power, that the Holy Spirit gave to the Church at Pentecost. We all have the same ability that the Spirit used to raise Jesus from the dead. Through the Spirit we all have the same power in us that created the universe. He is exactly the same Spirit with exactly the same nature and ability living in every believer. The Church is not a motley collection of spiritually impotent and impoverished weaklings: it is God's powerhouse, empowered with all the resource of heaven to fill this world with Jesus Christ. Through the Holy Spirit, the Church is full of the Kingdom power of its King: *For the kingdom of God is not a matter of talk but of power* (1Corinthians 4:20). When the Spirit comes into our lives he actually indwells us. He lives in us with all of his eternal God-life:

Since the Spirit of him who raised Jesus from the dead is living his life as God in you, he who raised

Christ from the dead will also give life to your mortal bodies through his Spirit, who lives his life as God in you. (Romans 8:11; author's translation)

Note this extremely important truth: when the Holy Spirit comes to live in us he does not come to help us live *our* lives. This is where so many Christians slip up and misunderstand what it means to be a Christian. The Holy Spirit does not live within you to assist you or guide you as you live your life. If I might put it bluntly: the Holy Spirit has no interest in your life. Yes, he loves you and cares for you. Nevertheless, I must emphasise that the reason for his indwelling you is not to help you live *your* life. To be in Christ means that Christ himself lives his life in and through your spirit by the Holy Spirit. Norman Grubb explains the Christian life thus: "It is Christ living his own divine life and fulfilling his own plans from before the foundation of the world in us." You and I have no life outside of Jesus Christ; Paul made this crystal clear:

I have been crucified with Christ and <u>I no longer live</u>, but Christ lives in me. The life I live in the body, I live by faith in the Son of God, who loved me and gave himself for me. (Galatians 2:20)

The Holy Spirit has only one life to live – his own God-life. His life is the life of Jesus, and of God the Father. The Holy Spirit is not the junior partner of the Trinity: to be filled with the Spirit is to be filled to all the measure of the fullness of God (Ephesians 3:19). The Holy Spirit lives his life as God in us; he does not reside in an area of our lives while we carry on trying to follow Jesus or live according to our own ideas. The Christian life is not difficult to live: it is impossible to live. This does not contradict what I said earlier about faith: that it is easy to live by faith. I said that God himself gives us all the faith we need to believe him. Christianity is all about God living his life in us. There is only One who can live the Christian life: Christ himself. Yet even Christ said: "I can do nothing on my own" (John 5:30). He was utterly reliant on the Father and the Spirit. He now lives his life in us through the same Holy Spirit. In order for the Elijah People to reach maturity we are obliged to allow the Holy Spirit to be Lord. Again, that might sound strange, when we correctly speak of Jesus as Lord. Paul, however, reminds us that: *The Lord is the Spirit, and where the Spirit of the Lord is, there is freedom* (2Corinthians 3:17).

We know that Jesus is not the Spirit and the Spirit is not Jesus. This verse means that Jesus is Lord and he expresses his Lordship on earth through the Spirit. Jesus reigns in heaven as King of kings and Lord of lords; he is the King of the Kingdom. His kingly reign, His Lordship, is administered and expressed on earth through the Holy Spirit. Where the Spirit is Lord, Jesus is Lord. Where Jesus is Lord, the Spirit is free to be himself. The freedom of the Spirit to be Lord establishes the Lordship of Jesus. Only those who have the Spirit as Lord have Jesus as Lord. All those who surrender to Jesus as Lord have the Spirit as Lord. They are those who are truly free. Therefore, the Elijah People fully understand their obligations and responsibilities to live according the Spirit:

Therefore, brothers, and sisters we have an obligation and responsibility—but it is not to the flesh, to live according to it and be controlled by it. For if you live according to the flesh, you will surely die; but if by the power of the indwelling Spirit within you, you practically put to death the misdeeds of the body, you will live, because those whose way of life is the Spirit of God are sons of God. (Romans 8:12-14 author's translation)

Spirit or flesh

The Elijah People do not live according to the flesh: that tendency in us towards self-gratification. The flesh is not the same as the sinful nature, which has been utterly removed from us in the new birth. Christians do not have two natures: a sinful nature and a new nature in Christ. The sinful nature has gone. The old sinful nature was all to do with being *in Adam*, and when we come to Christ the old person is gone: *If anyone is in Christ, he is a new creation; the old has gone, the new has come!* (2Corinthians 5:17). In Christ we are new creations; we have never existed before. Everything is brand new; we are born again. In the same way that a newborn baby has never existed before, so the new believer has a new existence: he has the nature of Christ through the indwelling of the Holy Spirit:

God made him who knew no sin to be sin for us, so that, in him we might become the righteousness of God. (2Corinthians 5:21)

Baptism in water then buries that old person. Baptism is a funeral with a difference. When we rise out of the 'grave' of the baptismal waters we are raised to a new life: the resurrection life of Jesus! We have the new nature of Christ within us in all his fullness through the Holy Spirit. If we do not live filled with the Holy Spirit then the flesh – our human self-gratification and way of life – will control us. Therefore, we submit to the life of the Holy Spirit and allow him to live his life as God in us. We do not live for ourselves and seek to gratify ourselves. The New Testament lists the works or the way of life of the flesh:

The works of the flesh are obvious: sexual immorality, impurity and debauchery; idolatry and witchcraft; hatred, discord, jealousy, fits of rage, selfish ambition, dissensions, factions and envy; drunkenness, orgies and the like. I warn you as I did before, that those who live like this will not inherit the kingdom of God. (Galatians 5:19-21)

Remember, Paul was writing to Christians here, not unbelievers. He reminded them that this way of life is totally unacceptable for Christians. He does not grade these works of the flesh: jealousy and hatred are just as bad as sexual immorality and witchcraft. This kind of lifestyle is not in keeping with being sons of God, who have a different way of life. The way of life of the sons of God is the Spirit; the Spirit is Lord of the sons of God, who produce the life of Christ, which is the fruit of the Spirit:

But the fruit of the Spirit is love, joy, peace, patience, kindness, goodness, faithfulness, gentleness and self-control. Against such things there is no law. Those who belong to Christ Jesus have crucified the flesh with its passions and desires. Since we live by the

Spirit, let us keep in step with the Spirit. Let us not become conceited, provoking and envying each other. (Galatians 5:22-26)

Note that Paul does not say the *fruits* of the Spirit; he says the *fruit* of the Spirit. This is the way of life of the Spirit: to produce Christ in us. This fruit is the character of Christ. We cannot say of ourselves that we find it difficult to love but we are faithful. Neither can we say that we are kind but find joy hard to achieve. That is nonsense. The character of Christ, the life of the Spirit is not something we carve up into segments. The Spirit's fruit is Jesus; and where the Spirit is Lord, Jesus' character is expressed in all its fullness. As we live in obedience to the Spirit as Lord he produces his fruit in us in increasing measure. This process continues through the whole of our earthly life. We are constantly being changed from one degree of glory to another, being transformed more and more into the likeness of Jesus (2Corinthians 3:18). We are constantly being restored to God's ultimate intention for us: to display the glory of God – Jesus – in all his fullness.

I have translated Romans 8:14 as 'those whose way of life is the Spirit are the sons of God'. That is its literal meaning. Other translations have the words 'led' or 'guided' by the Spirit, which are also accurate. The Greek word is used many times in the New Testament to mean '*led*'. However, the root of the term means a leading or guidance that leads to a destination, or a destiny. This word comes from another term which means a way of life; conduct; education; discipline; a course of life. Paul used it to describe himself:

You, however, know all about my teaching, <u>my way</u> <u>of life</u>, my purpose, faith, patience, love, endurance, persecutions, and sufferings. (2Timothy 3:10-11)

Paul's way of life was the Spirit of sonship. He was not embarrassed about it or reluctant to remind Timothy of the fact. That is why he could encourage Timothy and the New Testament Church to imitate him, to live like he did. He was an example of maturing sonship for them, through his relationship and fellowship with the Spirit of Jesus. In the same way we as the Elijah People should be able to say: 'If you want to know what Jesus is like, take a look at us'.

The true sons of God, the Elijah People, are those whose way of life is the Spirit. The Spirit's way of life in us is to fill us with the life of Christ, not only to redeem us and guarantee our place in heaven. The Spirit's way of life is to bring us to maturity as sons of our Father. His way of life is to bring the Father's plan and purpose for his Son to be fulfilled in and through us. To be led or guided by the Spirit is not like being led around on a leash like a dumb animal without any sense of direction or meaning. Neither is being led by the Spirit a guessing game in which we struggle in our attempts to discern the will of God our Father. Being led by the Spirit is to have the Spirit live his way of life in us as Lord. It is God's intention for each of his Elijah People to live this way.

The only way

God designed humanity to live in fellowship with him, filled with the Holy Spirit. It is abnormal for a Christian not to be filled with the Spirit of the living God. In fact, we have to go as far as to say that to be a non-Christian is totally unnatural. God created humanity to know him. The New Testament apostles and writers would be amazed by some of the theologies of the Holy Spirit that pervade the modern Church. For them, every Christian was born of the Spirit and baptised in the Holy Spirit. Speaking in tongues and regular, everyday use of the gifts of the Holy Spirit – both those in Romans 12 and 1Corinthians 12 – were normal Christian experiences, not an optional extra or the prerogative and privilege of so-called 'Spirit-baptised believers' or 'charismatics'. (That word refers to the gifts of the Spirit and literally means 'gifts of grace'). It is tragic that we differentiate between Christians who have the Spirit and those who don't. It is an utter nonsense to do so, and cannot be justified from the Bible's teaching on what it means to be a Christian. If you read the book of Acts properly you will discover that the apostles constantly searched for and emphasised the life of the Spirit among believers. Wherever and whenever they found a deficiency in the believers' experience of the Spirit, they immediately rectified it (see Acts 8:14-17 and Acts 19:1-6). They gauged anybody's genuineness of faith by the tangible evidence of the Spirit (see Acts 10:44-48). The centrality and importance of the Spirit is a constant theme throughout the Bible, right from the beginning. Have you ever noticed that the first Person of the Trinity mentioned in the Bible is the Spirit? Genesis 1:2 says that the 'Spirit of God was hovering over the waters'.

God's intention for Adam

Yahweh formed the man from the dust of the ground and breathed into his nostrils the breath of life, and the man became a living creature. (Genesis 2:7)

God's intention for Adam was that he be filled with the Spirit. Even though God formed him in preparation to live as God's son, Adam was useless until God breathed the Spirit into him; he breathed his life into him. God did not merely breathe oxygen into Adam with natural breath to bring him to physical life. He breathed his own breath, spiritual breath – the Holy Spirit – into him. Adam thus became a living creature, filled with the Spirit of God, alive in his spirit to his Father. Sadly, when Adam sinned he died. God had warned him:

"You must not eat of the tree of the knowledge of good and evil; because on the day you eat it you will surely die." (Genesis 2:17)

On the day Adam sinned he did not die physically; that came many years later. When he sinned, he died spiritually; he died in his spirit. He was no longer filled with the Spirit of God; he was spiritually dead. That was never God's intention for Adam; neither is it God's intention for us. We are created to be filled with his Spirit. When we are born again by the Holy Spirit, we are renewed in the image of God. We are spirit sons. Our restoration begins here, the moment we receive Jesus as Lord and are indwelt by the Holy Spirit. What Adam lost in his disobedience we recover through our obedience: fellowship with our Father through the Holy Spirit.

Zerubbabel the builder

In 538 BC, when the exiles began their return to Jerusalem after the Babylonian captivity, their leader, Zerubbabel, was instructed by God to rebuild the temple, a physical building. In a very famous passage, the prophet Zechariah received a word from the Lord to pass on to Zerubbabel concerning its construction:

This is the word of Yahweh to Zerubbabel: "Not by might, nor by power, but my Spirit," says Yahweh Almighty. (Zechariah 4:6)

This is a remarkable verse: even though he was constructing a physical building, Zerubbabel had to build it in a specific manner: by the Spirit. The word of the Lord was clear: he was not to build it by might or power, but only by the Spirit. He was not given several options and allowed to choose: he was categorically told, "Not by might nor by power." Might here is human efficiency, wealth, influence, prominence. Power means human strength or ability. All too often we are in danger of substituting the Spirit and replacing him with these things, under the guise of his prompting, direction and energy, wrongly attributing our endeavours as works of the Spirit. We end up with self-focused programmes, human initiatives, religious events, organisations and endless conferences on our personal development and ministry, instead of dynamic Spirit-originated and Spirit-empowered initiatives. If Zerubbabel had to build a physical building by the Spirit, how much more must we ensure that we build the spiritual house of God – the Church – in the same way.

Jesus the Anointed One

When Jesus lived on earth he came as God incarnate: fully God in human form. He was a real man and, at the same time, fully God. As God, Jesus could have performed miracles, signs and wonders, and healed the sick at any moment. He chose not to. He did no miracle, performed no sign or wonder, and healed no sick person, until something happened to him. He was filled with the Holy Spirit:

As Jesus was coming up out of the water, he saw heaven being torn open and the Spirit descending on him like a dove. (Mark 1:10)

Why did Jesus not do any of these things, even though he was able to do so as God? Because he wanted to show us how a person filled with the Holy Spirit lives; what a Spirit-filled man or woman can achieve; to demonstrate to us the way God had always planned for us to live. It is interesting to note that when Jesus went home after being filled with the Holy Spirit, his friends and neighbours noticed something different about him:

When the Sabbath came, Jesus began to teach in the synagogue, and many who heard him were amazed. "Where did this man get these things?" they asked. "What is this wisdom that has been given him, that he even does miracles? Isn't this the carpenter?" (Mark 6:2-3)

Jesus was the sinless Son of God; these people had known him all his life. Yet they noticed that he was different from the last time they had seen him. The difference was that he had been filled with the Holy Spirit. If Jesus chose to be filled with the Holy Spirit, demonstrating our absolute need of the same experience, and if he appeared different as a result of that experience, then the Elijah People are those who respond with the cry, "Fill us, Lord!"

The Church

At Pentecost, the Church began its mission and God-given mandate in the power, the dynamic ability, of the Holy Spirit: *They were all filled with the Holy Spirit, and spoke in other languages as the Spirit enabled them* (Acts 2:4). Ten days earlier Jesus had promised his disciples that they would be his witnesses – the living proof of his claims to be the risen and ascended King of kings, Lord of lords, and Saviour of the world. They would spread the Gospel of the Kingdom all over the world. But before they could do that, they had to wait until they had been baptised in the Spirit (Acts 1:5). Pentecost was their baptism, their initiation, into the realms of living by the Spirit. The world was never the same again.

The Church is qualified to call itself the Church only as it is faithful to this first initiation. We do not need another Pentecost; we just need to live in the reality of it. We cannot repeat Pentecost, but every believer needs the same initiation into the life of the Spirit as the one hundred and twenty experienced. Our experience of the Spirit cannot be any less than theirs, not if we believe in restoration. To experience less of the Spirit than they did means we have not even recovered what they had. Our calling as the Elijah People is to move beyond them in our fellowship with the Spirit and in our experience and measure of the Spirit. Never become nostalgic about Pentecost and the early chapters of the book of Acts. They were not the glory days of the Church. Just make sure that you have experienced your own personal Pentecost; that is the starting point for the Elijah People. Have you been baptised in the Holy Spirit? Are you living every day filled with the Spirit? Do you speak in tongues? Do you use the gifts of the Spirit?

Do you produce in increasing measure the fruit of the Spirit?

A House of the Spirit

As you come to him, the living Stone—rejected by men but chosen by God and precious to him— you also, like living stones, are being built into a spiritual house to be a holy priesthood, offering spiritual sacrifices acceptable to God through Jesus Christ. (1Peter 2:4-5)

The Church is a spiritual house: it is a house of the Spirit. If you were to come to my house, you would quickly recognise it as mine. You would see evidences of my life throughout the house: my clothes, my food, my possessions, my choices of décor, my values and my interests. My house represents me; in some ways you could say it 'looks' like me.

It is the same with the Church, the Elijah People. As the house of the Spirit, the Church 'looks' like the Spirit. It demonstrates the character of the Spirit. Let me go further and say that everything about the Church has the Spirit in it. Every expression of the house is spiritual, of the Spirit. Whenever and wherever the Church meets or expresses itself, everything is in the Spirit. Each structure and pattern of Church life is not based on habit or unjustifiable tradition: it is in the Spirit. Patterns of ministry and leadership are in the Spirit. Financial structures and practices of the house are in the Spirit. Praise and worship, and the ministry of the Word of God are in the Spirit. Those in leadership are men and women of the Spirit. The whole identity of the house and each expression of the house to the world are in the Spirit.

Every attitude and spoken word is in the Spirit. Together, as we live the life of the Spirit in fellowship with him and each other, we express the corporate life of the Spirit.

I do not intend to make a list of all the things the Church must be in the Spirit. Rather, let me encourage you to take a look at the expression of the house of the Spirit you belong to: the Church of which you are a member. Without being negatively critical, look at it through the eyes of the Spirit. Does it match up to God's status quo? Where you are empowered and enabled to make change, make it in line with the Word of God and the Spirit. You might come to realise that what you belong to bears no resemblance to the house of the Spirit. Get out of it as quickly as possible and find an expression of God's house that is worthy of him. Don't fritter your life away on something that is nothing to do with God and his purpose on earth.

Most of all, look at your own life in the Spirit. Allow him to speak to you about your own way of life. Where he encourages, you, be encouraged and determine to allow the Spirit to help you grow more to maturity. Where he challenges you and corrects you, repent and submit in loving obedience to his sanctifying work so that he might fashion you more and more, from glory to glory, into the likeness of the Lord Jesus, your elder brother. In this way you will bring honour to your Father and hasten the day of Jesus' return at the restoration of all things.

NINE

Turning Hearts

He will turn the hearts of the fathers to their children, and the hearts of the children to their fathers; or else I will come and strike the land with a curse. (Malachi 4:6)

And he will go on before the Lord, in the spirit and power of Elijah, to turn the hearts of the fathers to their children and the disobedient to the wisdom of the righteous—to make ready a people prepared for the Lord. (Luke 1:17)

We now need to concentrate on the mission of the Church as the Elijah People, though even here the qualities of such people still have a major emphasis. We are a sent people. God sent both Elijah and John the Baptist with a 'turning hearts' mission. If we read their stories without realising this important facet of their lives, we might conclude that they were callous, hardbitten men, who cared little for people. Nothing could be further from the truth. While they certainly were ruthless and not afraid to speak out and confront their hearers bluntly, their motivation was always to turn the hearts of those they addressed. This was evident even on Mount Carmel as Elijah called down fire from heaven:

"Answer me, Yahweh, answer me, so these people will know that you, Yahweh, are God, and that you are turning their hearts back again." (1Kings 18:37)

Elijah was not ultimately concerned that he be proved right and everybody else proved wrong. He was not consumed by his own reputation in this regard. He wanted everybody to know and recognise above all else that Yahweh was the living God; alongside that his longing and passion was that the people would turn their hearts again to God to love and serve him alone, as they had been created for. That was all he desired for them, even though his actions in attaining his objectives were admittedly radical and extreme. For example, he was utterly ruthless regarding the slaughter of the Baal-Melqart prophets at Mount Carmel. He did all he could possibly do to remove their evil influence from the people he cared so much for. Just like David killed the lion and the bear when they attacked his sheep (1Samuel 17:34-36), so Elijah fiercely protected God's flock by destroying those who sought to destroy them. Elijah could not have achieved his stated aim any other way. This demonstrates how important it was for Elijah to convey the message of the turned heart. He so desired the people of God to turn back to God he removed from their midst those who led them astray. He was a true shepherd of God's people. We must never forget that.

Come near to me

Both Elijah and John the Baptist welcomed people to themselves. Despite their radicalism and uncompromising stance for righteousness and truth, they accepted people with open arms. At times it seems they drove people away from them by their message and actions; we must admit that on occasions Jesus himself also appeared to do the same. In fact, all they were doing was to point out the stark contrast between God's plan for his people compared to the sinful ways they chose to live in and what they accepted as their status quo. Elijah, John the Baptist and Jesus were men who laid the demands of God in vivid, uncompromising ways before people. What is fascinating is despite these extreme measures, people were inexorably drawn to them. There is a beautiful moment in the account of that historic day on Mount Carmel. After the prophets of Baal-Melqart had spent all those hours frantically trying to get their non-existent god to send fire, Elijah stepped forward and spoke to the people who had gathered there to witness the spectacle. He reached out to them:

Elijah said to all the people, "Come near to me." And all the people came near to him. (1 Kings 18:30)

This tender incident captures the heart of Elijah, and, therefore, the heart of God towards people. Elijah did not hold them at arm's length, treating them as pariahs; he called them to himself, inviting them to come near to him. His heart went out to them; Elijah had the same heart attitude as Jesus, who was almost constantly besieged by vast numbers of people, despite the radical message he carried and embodied:

When he saw the crowds, he had compassion on them, because they were harassed and helpless, like sheep without a shepherd. (Matthew 9:36)

John the Baptist had the same heart too. The Gospels tell us that fairly soon after he began to preach his powerful message of repentance and the forgiveness of sins in preparing the way for the One to come: *People went out to him from Jerusalem and all Judea and the whole region of the Jordan* (Matthew 3:5). John did not drive the crowds away. It is true, as we have already stated, that he spoke strongly and directly to them. But he welcomed them to himself; he baptised them, he involved himself in the predicaments and situations of real people. Both Elijah and John the Baptist demonstrated the heart of the Gospel in their attitude of turning hearts. In this they were foreshadowing Jesus' own mission and heart towards his world: *"Come to me, all you who are weary and burdened, and I will give you rest"* (Matthew 11:28).

Reconciled and restored

What does this phrase – turning the hearts of fathers to children and children to fathers – mean? Of course, where necessary, it means the literal turning of real fathers to their children and real children to their fathers. However, if we look at the context closely it means more than that. When Elijah prayed on Mount Carmel he declared that God was turning the hearts of the people back to himself: the people were returning to God. That is what they did when they cried out in response to the fire: "Yahweh – he is God!" In their repentance they were reconciled to God and their relationship with him was restored. Malachi also mentioned that if hearts did not turn, the consequence would be a curse for them. When somebody is reconciled to God through faith in Jesus, the curse of sin is miraculously broken:

Christ redeemed us from the curse of the law by becoming a curse for us, for it is written: "Cursed is everyone who is hung on a tree." (Galatians 3:13)

The removal of the curse of sin by Jesus on the Cross opened the way for us to be reconciled to God our Father:

For God was pleased to have all his fullness dwell in him, and through him to reconcile to himself all things, whether things on earth or things in heaven, by making peace through his blood, shed on the cross. (Colossians 1:19-20)

If anyone is in Christ, he is a new creation; the old has gone, the new has come! All this is from God, who reconciled us to himself through Christ and gave us the ministry of reconciliation: that God was reconciling the world to himself in Christ, not counting men's sins against them. And he has committed to us the message of reconciliation. (2Corinthians 5:17-19)

Gabriel's declaration of John the Baptist's forthcoming ministry added something else to what Malachi had said: John would 'turn the hearts of the disobedient to the wisdom of the righteous' (Luke 1:17). People would leave their sinful, disobedient way of life and become righteous. Again, this describes what happens to us when we receive Jesus as Lord: our old sinful, disobedient nature dies and we receive the righteousness of Jesus, who is the wisdom of God

(1Corinthians 1:24). Turning hearts, therefore, is all to do with reconciliation and restoration: when we respond to the Gospel, repent of our sin (repentance has the idea of turning around to go in the opposite direction), turn away from our old life and put our faith in Jesus, we are miraculously reconciled to our Heavenly Father, and we begin our life of restoration.

Heart of the matter

The Elijah People have turned their hearts: towards God, towards themselves, and towards others. As such they are a people actively involved in reconciliation and restoration. This heart attitude is practically expressed in love, grace, mercy, forgiveness, justice and kindness. Inevitably, a heart that is reconciled to God will also do all that is possible to be reconciled to others; relationships are restored when hearts turn. While the Elijah People are those who never compromise their revelation, are dogged in their determination, and who constantly challenge the status quo, their attitude in doing so is always one of reconciliation and restoration out of a heart of love. They live with a redemptive attitude. Only a turned, changed heart can live like this. Therefore, we need to explain what the Bible means by the heart, since it uses the word to describe something very important about us, and we are warned: *above all else, guard your heart, for it is the wellspring of life* (Proverbs 4:23).

The word *heart* occurs several hundred times in the Bible. We also use the word as an idiom frequently in English: we wear our heart on our sleeve; we have a heart to heart; we get to the heart of something; we are one in heart; we capture a heart; we break hearts; we have aching hearts; we tell others to eat their heart out; we can have a heart of gold or stone; our hearts are in our mouths; we have our hearts in the right place; home is where the heart is. And, as the song says: we can even leave our heart in San Francisco!

Your heart is the centre, or the controlling factor of your life. It describes what you are really like deep down: it is what 'makes you tick'; it is the centre of your thoughts, moral values and attitudes. Your heart is the seat of your emotions, your feelings and desires. It is where you exercise your will and make your decisions. It controls and determines your mind and conscience. The heart is the inner person; the real you; the person you are when nobody else is around, when you are all alone. Your heart is who you really are. Whoever or whatever controls your heart controls you. When you become a Christian you have a heart transplant; you receive a new heart. The old, sinful one is not cleaned; it is replaced. Describing what happens to us in the new birth, God spoke through Ezekiel:

> *I will give you a new heart and put a new spirit in you; I will remove from you your heart of stone and give you a heart of flesh. And I will put my Spirit in you and move you to follow my decrees and be careful to keep my laws. (Ezekiel 36:26-27)*

The greatest commandment

Your new heart, which the Holy Spirit gives you in your new birth, is the heart of Christ; therefore it is designed to fulfil what Jesus described as the greatest commandment. One day, Jesus was asked one of the most important questions anybody ever asked him while he was on earth. He responded by talking about the heart:

> An expert in the law tested Jesus with this question: "Teacher, which is the greatest commandment in the Law?" Jesus replied: "'Love the Lord your God with all your heart and with all your soul and with all your mind.' This is the first and greatest commandment. And the second is like it: 'Love your neighbour as yourself.' All the Law and the Prophets hang on these two commandments."
> (Matthew 22:35-40)

Jesus said that the Law of Moses, in fact the whole of the Old Testament, is all about love, and, in particular, love for God, love for oneself and love for one's neighbour. Jesus' questioner was concerned about doing the right thing, about keeping commandments. Like many others, he thought that doing what was right made one right with God. As E. Stanley Jones pointed out: "The kingdom of God is concerned with what you are. The kingdoms of this world are concerned with what you do." Jesus was concerned about *being* right, about who and what we *are*. He got to the very heart of things. To demonstrate this he went to the essential nature, or the heart, of the Law. He took the entire Law of Moses, and brought it down to two statements. That is why Jesus' reply to the question was amazing. Contrary to the questioner's expectation, he made no reference to the Ten Commandments. Instead, Jesus referred to this passage:

> Hear, O Israel: Yahweh our God, Yahweh is one. Love Yahweh your God with all your heart and

with all your soul and with all your strength. These
commandments that I give you today are to be
upon your hearts. (Deuteronomy 6:4-6)

Verse four is one of the most important verses in the
entire Word of God. It describes the fundamental
revelation of God: he is one. There is only one God.
Remember we have established this was at the very heart
of Elijah's message: Yahweh was the living God. For the
Elijah People this means Jesus is the living Lord. That is
the basis of the Ten Commandments: 'you will have no
other gods besides me' (Exodus 20:3). Our relationship
to this one God was and is eternally destined to be one
of our love for him from our hearts. Verse six tells us that
God's intention for his Law is that it will be written upon
or in our hearts. It will be internalised within us in a love
relationship with God. It was never destined to remain
an external set of regulations, set on tablets of stone. It
was given to be written on the tablet of the heart.

Sandwiched between these two statements is the heart
of everything. Jesus said the greatest commandment is to
love God with all your heart, with all your soul and with
all your strength. Jesus went deep – into their hearts –
and simply said, "Love God with all that you are." Then
he went even deeper and quoted a verse from Leviticus,
which says:

Do not seek revenge or bear a grudge against one
of your people, but love your neighbour as yourself.
I am Yahweh. (Leviticus 19:18)

This little verse, tucked away in all the various
religious, moral, medical, social and ethical laws

contained in Leviticus was taken up by its Author, Jesus Christ, to signify the real meaning of all the other laws, and the practical outworking and proof of our love for God: love your neighbour as yourself.

Jesus put these two statements together: Love God with all your heart, and love your neighbour in the same way as you love yourself. Then he dropped a bombshell and in effect said, "All the Bible rests on these two commandments!" Imagine that: every one of the sixty-six books – every verse, every doctrine, every story, every Psalm and Proverb, every prophecy – hangs on the command to love God, love ourselves, and love everybody else like we love God and ourselves. Turning hearts is the most powerful message we have to carry as the Elijah People. The proof of a turned heart, therefore, is love, specifically the God kind of love. It is a love that is expressed with the attitude of reconciliation. As the Elijah People, our new 'turned' hearts are enabled to love in precisely the same way as God loves: *We love because he first loved us* (1John 4:19). Our new heart of love expresses itself in three directions:

1. Towards God

The Elijah People are first and foremost lovers of God. That might sound strange: to have to accentuate the fact that Christians are meant to love God. It should be the most normal and basic thing Christians are: lovers of God. Nevertheless, it has to be said. Jesus' accusation against the Church in Ephesus was startling:

You have persevered and have endured hardships for my name, and have not grown weary. Yet I hold this against you: You have forsaken your first love. Remember the height from which you have fallen! Repent and do the things you did at first. If you do not repent, I will come to you and remove your lampstand from its place. (Revelation 2:3-5)

One of the major, leading Churches of the New Testament, despite all its revelation, reputation, perseverance and prominence, had fallen from a great height. The people had forsaken their first love – they no longer loved the Lord in the way they used to. Jesus' appeal and warning to the believers in Ephesus was clear: "You do lots of things for me and in my name. You are willing to suffer for me and my honour. You are prepared to stand up for what is right. You are rightly concerned about truth and exposing the fraudulent claims of those false apostles. You do many things well. But you fail in the most important thing: you don't love me anymore. I am no longer your passion. I want you to love me like you used to."

This takes us back to an earlier chapter when we looked at the conversation between the resurrected Jesus and Peter as they walked along the shore of Galilee. Remember how Jesus asked Peter that life-changing question: *"Do you love me more than these?"* (John 21:15). All Jesus wanted to know was whether Peter loved him more than anyone and anything else. If the answer were yes, everything else would slot into place and have the right priority. Peter's love for Jesus was all that mattered to Jesus. The greatest thing we can do for God is to love him. He does not need our love; he is not inadequate or incomplete unless we love him. There is no void in God that is filled only when we love him. He just wants us to love him, and that all that we do for him subsequently flows from that love. Jesus said:

"As the Father has loved me, so have I loved you. Now remain in my love. If you obey my commands, you will remain in my love, just as I have obeyed my Father's commands and remain in his love." (John 15:9-10)

It is possible for a Christian to obey and serve the Lord Jesus Christ solely out of duty or habit: after all, he is the Lord and he must be obeyed. He deserves to be obeyed and served. However, that kind of lifestyle and relationship with God will become arduous, and life will become legalistic: a set of rules and self-imposed laws and religious habits. The person whose heart is filled with love for God obeys and serves him simply out of love: "I love the Lord and only want to bring him pleasure." Jim Elliot, one of five young American missionaries martyred in the jungles of Ecuador in 1956, wrote in his journal of his love for the Lord:

I care not if I never raise my voice again for him, if only I may love him, please him. Mayhap in mercy he shall give me a host of children that I may lead them through the vast star fields to explore his delicacies whose finger-ends set them to burning. But if not, if only I may see him, touch his garments, and smile into his eyes – ah then, not stars nor children shall matter, only himself.

Elliot's love of his Lord and Saviour meant he was prepared to lay down his life in the jungles of Ecuador at the relatively young age of twenty-eight, for the sake of those he was attempting to reach with the Gospel of the love of God. Why? Because he had learned the secret that: *Love is as strong as death* (Song of Solomon 8:6). The first members of the tribe to believe in the Lord Jesus were those who had killed Elliot and his companions. After their conversion to Christ they told of how the missionaries refused to fight back when attacked, even though they were armed with rifles against spears. Rather, they allowed themselves to be killed instead of retaliating and killing those who could have otherwise gone to hell. That is true love.

2. Towards yourself

This is probably the aspect of the greatest commandment that Christians struggle with, because it seems to go against everything they believe a Christian should be: humble; not consumed with self; to live with a constant sense of one's unworthiness; self-denial; sin-consciousness; even self-loathing. Furthermore, the Word of God itself warns that: *In the last days…people will be lovers of themselves* (2Timothy 3:1-2).

To love your neighbour as you love yourself is not the same thing as Paul is talking about here when he warns against those who love themselves. These particular individuals are not godly at all: they take advantage of vulnerable people and destroy the lives of others. They are concerned only with self-promotion, selfish ambition, self-adoration, and self-absorption. To love your neighbour as you love yourself is quite another thing. Before we are able to accept and love others, we have to learn to love and accept ourselves. The order of the greatest commandment is important: love for God is

the overriding principle for everything else. As the
Scripture quoted earlier says: *We love because he first
loved us* (1John 4:19).

If I can accept the fact that God loves and accepts me,
then surely I must be able to accept – and love – myself.
If God does not condemn me, then I must not condemn
myself. If God likes me, then I must like myself. If God
thinks I am worth loving, then I must be worth loving. If
God chose me before the foundation of the world to be
his son, then I must have some significance in the world's
history. The Elijah People are not arrogant, but they have
arrived at the point in their lives in which they know that
they are not unworthy sinners, whose destiny in life is
not to grovel around from crisis to crisis, always full of
self-doubt and laden with inferiority complexes. Far too
many Christians enjoy holding 'pity parties' for
themselves in which they wallow in the lie of how
unworthy they are. It is inverted pride and brings no
honour to Jesus.

The Elijah People look in the mirror and like what
they see: those re-created in the image of God, chosen
by God, forgiven by God, loved by God, those who are
at peace with God, and through whom God is making
Jesus known to the world. That is how we should
see ourselves, because that is the way our Heavenly
Father sees us. And the Holy Spirit within us agrees
with the Father. In and through Christ we are the
answer for the world, not the cause of its problems. If
Christians truly believed who they are in Christ, the
Church would cease to be an insular self-help clinic and
become God's expression of love and power to a sin-sick
world.

3. Towards others

Love your neighbour as you love yourself. The way you behave towards others is directly linked to how you love God and yourself. Jesus said:

"In everything, do to others what you would have them do to you, for this sums up the Law and the Prophets." (Matthew 7:12)

This is often called the Golden Rule: even non-Christian scholars and philosophers widely agree that this is the ideal way to live. However, outside of a relationship with God through Jesus, it is impossible. Jesus said that, practically, treating others in the way that you would like them to treat you fulfils the greatest commandment. Behave towards others in the same way you would like them to behave towards you. Speak to people, and speak about people, in the same way you would like to be spoken to, in the same way you would like to be spoken about. The entire Old Testament (the Law and the Prophets) is about just this one thing. Our love of God is not theoretical; it is intensely practical: how we treat other people really matters. It is the proof and essence of our love for God, that our hearts are turned. This theme runs right through the New Testament:

Love does no harm to its neighbour. Therefore love is the fulfilment of the law. (Romans 13:10)

The entire law is summed up in a single command: 'Love your neighbour as yourself'. (Galatians 5:14)

If you really keep the royal law found in Scripture, 'Love your neighbour as yourself,' you are doing right. (James 2:8)

Many times you will discover in the New Testament the phrase 'one another' or 'each other', indicating how Christians behave towards each other. Here is just one example:

Now that you have purified yourselves by obeying the truth so that you have sincere love for your brothers, love one another deeply, from the heart. (1Peter 1:22)

In one of his most explosive teachings, Jesus set the pattern that would authenticate the Church's Gospel message to the world. He talked about our love for each other and its consequent impact on the world: *"By this all men will know that you are my disciples: if you love one another"* (John 13:35). Jesus said that what will convince the world of his claims to be the Lord and Saviour of the world, of the authenticity of our mission and message, and the right to be heard, would not only be the power of preaching, signs and wonders, good works, faith, mission strategies and evangelistic initiatives, or the many other things that comprise our Gospel. The one thing that will convince the world more than anything else will be the fact that we as the Elijah People genuinely love one another. That is why Paul said of love: *These three remain: faith, hope and love. But the greatest of these is love* (1Corinthians 13:13). Commenting on John 13:34-35, Francis Schaeffer said:

According to Jesus himself, the world has the right to decide whether we are true Christians, true disciples of Christ, on the basis of the love we show to all true Christians. John 17:21 provides something even more sobering in that here Jesus gives the world the right to judge whether the Father has sent the Son, on the basis of whether the world sees observable love among all true Christians.

I must also affirm most forcibly that the power and demonstration of God's love is not confined to the Church; we do not limit our love only to our fellow brothers and sisters in Christ. Probably the best-known verse in the entire Bible says:

For God so loved the world that he gave his Only Begotten Son, that whoever believes on him should not perish but have everlasting life. (John 3:16)

God's love is not limited to his children; he does not only love Christians. He loves all people. The love that we as the Elijah People demonstrate to each other is not restricted to the Church. I agree that in the Church the love of God is expressed to each other in a special way. But that love also overflows to the world. We love all people with the love of God. Even though the Church stands in stark contrast to the world and refuses to accept its status quo, its values, its rules and morals, the Church's attitude to the world is always one of love and hope. I cannot stress too highly that God the Father did not send Jesus into the world to condemn it, but to save the world (John 3:17). The attitude of the Elijah People to the world is, therefore, *never* condemnatory but at all times redemptive. It is inevitable that the lifestyle and message of the Elijah People will convict the world, will make the world uncomfortable and angry, and will even cause people to be hostile towards us. It is the nature of the Gospel to do that – it is offensive to the sinner (Galatians 5:11). Nevertheless, the carriers of the Gospel are radical in their love for sinners as well as in their fierce, uncompromising stand for the glory of Jesus. Our mission is to convey the love of God to his world and so establish his status quo. God's love is the motivation for our mission. Francis Schaeffer expressed this so beautifully:

> *Love is not an easy thing; it is not just an emotional urge; but an attempt to move over and sit in the other person's place and see how his problems look to him. Love is a genuine concern for the individual...To be engaged in personal 'witness' as a duty or because our Christian circle exerts a social pressure on us, is to miss the whole point. The reason we do it is that this one before us is the image-bearer of God, and he is an individual who is unique in the world.*

Our love for God and our love for his world, therefore, are not mutually exclusive. We love God with a passion and we love his world with the same passion. Jesus loved people, all kinds of people. He mixed with prostitutes, lepers, political zealots, collaborators, business people, children, farmers, soldiers, fishermen, and the social and political elite. He loved them all. It is true that not all of them reciprocated that love, but that was not the point. Jesus loved people unconditionally, because God is love. The old adage is true: God loves sinners but hates sin. We must differentiate between the two. We hate what people are – they are sinners. Nevertheless, we love them even though they are sinners. That is why Jesus said this is the greatest commandment, because only God loves like that. In Christ, so do we.

The power of forgiveness

Biblical reconciliation – turning hearts – inevitably and necessarily involves forgiveness. Reconciliation is the outcome of forgiveness. Reconciliation implies that a relationship has broken down or been damaged: somebody, through actions, attitudes or words – or all three – has caused estrangement and separation. Hearts have turned away from each other and need to be turned back in reconciliation. In reconciliation, somebody asks for forgiveness and somebody grants it. Reconciliation turns hearts towards each other.

Both Elijah and John the Baptist preached reconciliation with God through repentance and forgiveness. God's heart had never turned away from his people and his world; but people had turned away in their hearts from him. Therefore, Elijah and John preached a repentance that would result in God's forgiveness. It is impossible to preach repentance and reconciliation without offering forgiveness. In order to turn people's hearts, Elijah and John the Baptist encouraged and urged their hearers to repent, to ask God for forgiveness, and God would gladly forgive them. God's forgiveness is a demonstration of his love, grace and mercy:

When you were dead in your sins and in the uncircumcision of your sinful nature, God made

you alive with Christ. He forgave us all our sins,
having cancelled the written code, with its
regulations, that was against us and that stood
opposed to us; he took it away, nailing it to the
cross. (Colossians 2:13-14)

God's nature is to forgive all sins: he is never reluctant
to act in forgiveness when we repent and ask him to
forgive. He is more prepared to forgive than we are to ask
him for his forgiveness. It is God's character to forgive:

If my people, who are called by my name, will
humble themselves and pray and seek my face and
turn from their wicked ways, then will I hear from
heaven and will forgive their sin and will heal their
land. (2Chronicles 7:14)

When God forgives he chooses not to remember our
sin ever again. He will never call it to mind. In that sense
he 'forgets'. The Bible makes it very clear that when God
forgives our sins he does not remember them anymore:

"This is the covenant I will make with the house of
Israel after that time," declares Yahweh. "I will put
my law in their minds and write it on their hearts. I
will be their God, and they will be my people…"For
I will forgive their wickedness and will remember
their sins no more." (Jeremiah 31:33-34)

The writer to the Hebrews takes up this passage from
Jeremiah twice (Hebrews 8:8-13; 10:16-18) to emphasise
that this is the covenant we live in now as Christians.
The New Covenant in Christ means that God has forgiven

all our sins and no longer remembers them. They are gone! Does that mean that our past sins are actually erased from God's memory? If that is the case then he does not know everything that has ever happened. Of course he can remember our sins; God has a perfect memory and perfect knowledge. He is all-knowing (omniscient). Nothing goes out of his mind as if he suffers some form of amnesia. What it means is that God does not deal with us through the filter of our previous sinful life:

> *For as high as the heavens are above the earth, so great is his love for those who fear him; as far as the east is from the west, so far has he removed our transgressions from us. (Psalm 103:11-12)*

God chooses never to bring back up before us what we used to be. For him, it has gone and is no longer an issue. He does not think, "There's Roger, who used to be this or that, who used to do this or that." He does not see me as an ex-sinner or as an ex-anything. He sees me and treats me only as a righteous son and deals with me solely on the basis of who I am in Christ. When the Bible says that God will remember my sins no more, it means they are no longer a barrier between us. He will never raise them again, because they no longer exist. He will not even discuss them with me. If I were to bring up my sinful past life with him, his response would be, "What are you talking about?"

It is the same if I sin as a believer. My nature is to live to please my heavenly Father; it is not inevitable that I will sin. I do not face each new day with dread, worried about all the sins I might or might not commit during the day. I am a saint with the nature of Jesus in me in all his fullness through the indwelling Holy Spirit. I sin only when

I choose to do so: when I allow the flesh to dominate. If I sin, I am always able to approach my gracious and merciful Father in repentance. This is what happens when I do so: *If we confess our sins he is faithful and just and will forgive us our sins* (1John 1:9). This is the power of God's forgiveness. He forgives swiftly and gladly; and the result of his forgiveness is my reconciliation with him. Whatever it was in me that caused his displeasure, grief and even anger, is gone and forgotten. It is as if it never happened. God does not keep it in his back pocket and bring it out if I sin again, because: *Love keeps no record of wrongs* (1Corinthians 13:5).

Forgive and forget

The way God forgives us is exactly the way we forgive each other. Unforgiveness is a cancer that eats away at the hearts of people. Galatians 5:15 says: *If you keep on biting and devouring each other, watch out or you will be destroyed by each other.* Some are totally unwilling to forgive those who have done them harm, preferring to harbour bitterness and hatred (which often accompany unforgiveness) towards the person who mistreated them or sinned against them. Others say, "I can forgive but I can't forget", meaning that they will always remember the harm done to them and will use it as a shield of protection or a weapon of revenge in the future. Neither of these ways is acceptable for the Elijah People. I am not downplaying some of the horrific things done to people. The appalling suffering by, and the unimaginable physical and psychological damage and abuse done to innocent people is evil and, in many cases, too awful to imagine. Nevertheless, the message of turning hearts means we are miraculously able as the Elijah People to be those who live forgiven and forgiving, no matter what we have done to others or what others have done to us.

Jesus and the writers of the New Testament were well aware of the power of forgiveness and of the power of unforgiveness. Therefore, there is much emphasis on the necessity for us to always forgive one another:

As God's chosen people, holy and dearly loved, clothe yourselves with compassion, kindness, humility, gentleness and patience. Bear with each other and forgive whatever grievances you may have against one another. Forgive as the Lord forgave you. And over all these virtues put on love, which binds them all together in perfect unity. (Colossians 3:12-14)

"If you forgive men when they sin against you, your heavenly Father will also forgive you. But if you do not forgive men their sins, your Father will not forgive your sins." (Matthew 6:14-15)

"When you stand praying, if you hold anything against anyone, forgive him, so that your Father in heaven may forgive you your sins." (Mark 11:25)

"If your brother sins against you, rebuke him, and if he repents, forgive him." (Luke 17:3)

Jesus graphically explained the importance of forgiveness in response to a question that Peter asked him:

"Lord, how many times shall I forgive my brother when he sins against me? Up to seven times?"

Jesus answered, "I tell you, not seven times, but seventy times seven." (Matthew 18:21-22)

Peter thought he was being generous in his estimation of forgiveness. Jesus showed him he was wide of the mark. 'Seventy times seven' means there is no limit to the times you forgive somebody. Jesus then explained what he meant by telling his disciples the parable of the unmerciful servant: a man whose master forgave him a debt of millions of pounds, but who then immediately refused to forgive his fellow servant who owed him only a few hundred pounds (Matthew 18:21-35). The unmerciful servant was hauled back before his master who sent him to jail until he repaid the master all his own debt. The man's unwillingness to have mercy on his fellow servant and grant him forgiveness cost him his own forgiveness and freedom. Jesus warned: *"This is how my heavenly Father will treat each of you unless you forgive your brother from your heart"* (Matthew 18:35).

There is the heart again. We have no choice but to forgive from our heart those who ask for our forgiveness. We must forgive as the Lord forgave us, from the heart, because we love in the same way that he loves. You cannot love like the Lord and not forgive like the Lord. Note that there is also a direct correlation between our forgiveness of others and the Lord's forgiveness of us. If we refuse to forgive those who sin against us, then the Lord will not forgive us. We can come to him and ask him to forgive us of our sins, but if we hold unforgiveness towards anybody in our hearts, he will not forgive us. He will say, "Forgive that person and I will forgive you." We cannot expect God to behave in a manner that we refuse to behave in. We as the Elijah People are like him; therefore we forgive like him. We are heart people.

When you read the stories of Elijah and John the Baptist, never forget that they were men of great forgiveness and grace. Despite the terrible things said and done to them, they constantly and consistently held out the offering of forgiveness to all, even to those who opposed them. In fact, even Ahab himself, when he heard from Elijah the word of the Lord concerning his fate, humbled himself for a while (1Kings 21:27-29). God and Elijah responded to his act of humility by not bringing disaster on him in his lifetime. John the Baptist helped people find forgiveness with God; he told them what they needed to do and baptised them to effect their forgiveness (Luke 3:3-14). He offered forgiveness and then granted it on God's behalf.

Forgiveness has no memory

The heart of forgiveness is so powerful it forgives even when people do not ask for it. Even when those who have done you wrong do not ask for forgiveness, you are still able and willing to freely forgive them. Your heart is so filled with love, grace and mercy that you live free in your heart by forgiving even those who never ask for it. The most famous example in the Word of God, of course, is that of Jesus. As he hung on the Cross, he said to his Father: *"Father, forgive them, for they don't know what they are doing"* (Luke 23:34). If ever anybody could justify an unwillingness to forgive, it was Jesus, as he suffered and died as an innocent, sinless man, publically abused and degraded, in the most unimaginable pain, completely alone. As the prophet

Isaiah says: *He was despised and rejected by men; a man of sorrows and acquainted with grief* (Isaiah 53:3).

Yet even here Jesus freely and willingly forgave all those who slandered him, accused him, beat him, robbed him and killed him. He died a free man. The message of the Elijah People, those who are just like their Lord and elder brother Jesus, is a message of love, restoration, reconciliation, and forgiveness. This is what turning hearts is all about. Forgiveness has no memory. Forgiveness and reconciliation bring about restoration.

Let me conclude this chapter with a true story. A few years ago I watched a programme that commemorated the sixtieth anniversary of the liberation of Auschwitz. World leaders gathered in Cracow, Poland, to remember the day when the Russian Army freed the survivors of the Nazi death camp. The programme followed one particular little old lady's return to Auschwitz. She was only ten when she was liberated and had been imprisoned there with her twin sister, who also survived. These two sisters feature in a famous film clip of a line of twins being escorted out of the camp by Russian Army nurses on the day of liberation. Josef Mengele, the notorious doctor at Auschwitz, used twins for his evil experiments on humans, including this woman and her sister.

This little old lady was remarkable. As she shuffled around the snow-covered streets and buildings a reporter interviewed her. She held no bitterness or hatred towards those who committed these atrocities, even Mengele, but walked around that terrible place in tremendous dignity and peace. When asked how she could behave in such a way after all that had been done

172

to her, she spoke about forgiveness: that there was no point in hating those who so shamelessly abused and violated her all those years ago. If she had not forgiven them, her life would have been wasted, eaten away by her bitterness and refusal to forgive. She had chosen to live free. In a powerful statement she said, "Forgiveness is self-healing; it is a gift you make to yourself."

TEN

The Vital Breath

Elijah was a man just like us. He prayed earnestly that it would not rain, and it did not rain on the land for three and a half years. Again he prayed, and the heavens gave rain, and the earth produced its crops. (James 5:17-18)

When I was a student at Bible School, my Principal taught a course on the centrality of prayer in the life of the Church. He entitled it *The Vital Breath*. That phrase has stayed with me ever since: prayer is the vital breath of the Church. Prayer certainly was the vital breath for Elijah. It is highly significant that when the New Testament writers looked to an Old Testament figure to encourage the Church to pray, they turned to Elijah, the man 'just like us'.

Prayer is a central theme in Elijah's story. Earlier, we discovered that Elijah received the word of the Lord and then spoke it prophetically. It is important to state firmly that the word of the Lord did not come to him in a vacuum or without any reference to his relationship with God; it came through the time he spent in the presence of God in prayer. Everything Elijah spoke as prophecy had first of all been spoken to him by God as a direct result of his fellowship with God in prayer. When Elijah first challenged Ahab, his justification for doing so was because of his own relationship with God: *"As Yahweh, the God of Israel lives, before whom I stand"* (1Kings 17:1).

Elijah did not say that he had once stood in the presence of God, or that God had merely visited him solely for the specific purpose of bringing this word of judgement. No, he made it clear that Yahweh was not somebody whom he merely acknowledged as God: he said, "I stand before him in present reality; I live in the presence of God. I live in the place of prayer." It is evident that Elijah had been praying long before he went to Ahab to announce the judgement of God regarding the rain. James tells us that Elijah prayed earnestly that it would not rain. Some commentators suggest that the rain had already stopped falling long before Elijah went to Ahab, and that Elijah might well have been praying for up to six months prior to his prophetic declaration. One thing is certain: empty words did not flow from Elijah's lips. His prophecies emanated from his life of prayer. In that place of prayer, Elijah learned to listen and speak. In prayer he discovered the heartbeat and the heart cry of God.

Elijah prayed in a variety of ways in a variety of circumstances. As we have just observed, he had an overarching life of prayer in which he regularly and consistently spent time in God's presence. He put his prayer life into practice to considerable effect when he met the various situations he encountered. When the widow of Zarephath's son died Elijah took the boy in his arms and prayed:

He cried out to Yahweh, "Yahweh my God, have you brought tragedy also upon this widow I am staying with, by causing her son to die?" Then he stretched himself out on the boy three times and cried to Yahweh, "Yahweh my God, let this boy's life return to him!" (1Kings 17:20-21)

This was real, heartfelt prayer. Elijah was not concerned here with theological correctness or the right technique of prayer. He cried out to the God of life from the depth of his heart. Three times he stretched himself out over the boy and prayed intensely and earnestly a simple but specific prayer, imploring God: "let this boy's life return to him!" God responded to this kind of prayer; the boy came back to life.

Prayer played a significant part in Elijah's encounter with the prophets of Baal-Melqart at Mount Carmel. Elijah challenged the false prophets to hold a prayer meeting: *"You call on the name of your god, and I will call on the name of Yahweh"* (1Kings 18:24). In effect he said, "You pray to your invented, imaginary god and I will pray to the living God. I know what will happen because I have already been in prayer with the living God and he has told me this is what to do. The living God will answer my prayer." Later in the day, when the time came for God to act, Elijah prayed again so that everybody could hear to whom he was speaking and who was going to act in response to his prayer:

The prophet Elijah stepped forward and prayed: "Yahweh, God of Abraham, Isaac and Israel, let it be known today that you are God in Israel and that I am your servant and have done all these things at your command. Answer me, Yahweh, answer me, so these people will know that you,

Yahweh, are God, and that you are turning their hearts back again." (1Kings 18:36-37)

Even after the dramatic response of God to Elijah's prayer in the fire from heaven, the resulting exclamation of the people: "Yahweh, he is God!" and the slaughter of the Baal-Melqart prophets, prayer was not finished for Elijah that day. He still had another prayer to pray before his work was done. He climbed to the top of Mount Carmel, bent down to the ground and put his face between his knees. As James tells us: *again he prayed, and the heavens gave rain* (James 5:18). Seven times he prayed that the rain would come. Elijah had, in his heart, from his place of prayer, already heard the rain falling. He prayed until what he heard in prayer physically manifested in a heavy rain.

We see Elijah's prayer life again when he ran away from Jezebel. We have to admit that his first prayer was not one that God was about to answer in the way that Elijah wished: *"I have had enough, Yahweh," he said. "Take my life; I am no better than my ancestors"* (1Kings 19:4). I am glad the Bible records this part of Elijah's life and this prayer, because prayer must be honest; it is not a religious ritual that takes no account of our needs, emotions and feelings. Elijah could pray like this because he knew the God to whom he was praying. God knew that Elijah was under terrible stress and had had enough; his grace was about to go to work on him. Later in the chapter Elijah prayed again from the cave at Horeb in response to God's question: "What are you doing here?" Elijah prayed the burden of his heart, what he really felt about the situation in his nation. He prayed the same prayer twice:

"I have been very zealous for Yahweh, God Almighty. The Israelites have rejected your covenant, broken down your altars, and put your prophets to death with the sword. I am the only one left, and now they are trying to kill me too." (1Kings 19:10, 14)

Prayer and the early Church

There are over thirty-five references to prayer in the Acts of the Apostles. The early Elijah People knew the importance of prayer. Previously I stressed the importance of personal prayer in the life of the believer. We will never grow in our sonship unless or until we regularly pray and read the Word of God. However, the same is true corporately. The early Church demonstrates to us how vital prayer is, not only for the individual, but also for the corporate, for the Body of Christ. Let me highlight some of the references to prayer in the book of Acts. Note when they prayed, why they prayed, and how they prayed. Note, too, what happened through the prayers of the early Elijah People.

- Acts 1:14 – In the ten days between the ascension of Jesus and the coming of the Spirit at Pentecost, the believers 'all joined together constantly in prayer'.
- Acts 1:24 – When choosing who would replace Judas Iscariot among the apostles, they prayed, "Lord, you know everyone's heart. Show us who you have chosen."
- Acts 2:42 – Those three thousand new believers at Pentecost, who were added to the one hundred twenty, 'devoted themselves to the apostles' teaching and to the fellowship, to the breaking of bread and to prayer'.

- Acts 3:1 – The wonderful miracle that Peter and John performed with the crippled man took place when they were on their way to the Temple 'at the time of prayer'.
- Acts 4:24 – When Peter and John were released from prison and returned to the Church, the Church all 'raised their voices together in prayer to God'.
- Acts 4:31 – Such was the power in this prayer meeting, in which the Church asked God to increase the dynamic flow of the Spirit, 'the place where they were meeting was shaken. And they were all filled with the Holy Spirit and spoke the word of God boldly'.
- Acts 6:4 – When the dispute arose between the widows over food distribution, the apostles appointed seven spiritual men to resolve this vitally important issue that threatened the unity of the Church. They delegated the task to them because they had to give their attention to 'prayer and the ministry of the word'.
- Acts 6:6 – Before releasing the seven to their task, the apostles 'prayed and laid their hands on them'.
- Acts 7:59 – As Stephen was being martyred, 'he prayed, "Lord Jesus, receive my spirit."'
- Acts 8:15 – When the Gospel spread to Samaria through Philip, the apostles travelled there from Jerusalem to ensure that the new believers also experienced the baptism in the Holy Spirit: 'When they arrived, they prayed for them that they might receive the Holy Spirit'.
- Acts 9:11 – After Saul met Jesus on the Damascus road, Saul was unable to see. God spoke to a disciple in Damascus called Ananias and told him, "Go to the house of Judas on Straight Street and ask for a man from Tarsus named Saul, for he is praying."

- Acts 10:9 – While the messengers sent from Cornelius (who himself had been praying regularly) were on their way to get Peter, Peter, unaware of what was about to happen, 'went up on the roof to pray'. The result was that the Gospel broke out among the Gentiles.
- Acts 12:5,12 – When persecution broke out against the Church in Jerusalem, 'Peter was thrown into prison, but the Church was earnestly praying to God for him'. As a result of the Church's prayer, an angel rescued Peter, who went to the house of Mary, John's mother, where 'many people had gathered and were praying'.
- Acts 13:3 – When Paul and Barnabas were sent from Antioch on their first apostolic mission, they did so only after their fellow ministries had 'fasted and prayed...and placed their hands on them'.
- Acts 14:23 – When Paul and Barnabas appointed elders in each of the new Churches they did so 'with prayer and fasting'.
- Acts 16:25 – When Paul and Barnabas were arrested and thrown into jail in Philippi, instead of complaining and arguing they were 'praying and singing hymns to God'. God responded and caused an earthquake, which resulted in the salvation of the jailer and all his family.
- Acts 28:8 – After Paul was shipwrecked on Malta he went to the home of Publius, whose father was there, suffering from dysentery: 'Paul went in to see him and, after prayer, placed his hands on him, and healed him'. As a result the rest of the sick on the island came to Paul and all of them were healed.

The early Church knew how to pray, and the effectiveness of their praying is well documented here. Jesus himself had taught them to pray. The apostles had lived with him for over three years and had observed his life at first hand. Such was the centrality of prayer in Jesus' life that eventually they asked him, *"Lord, teach us to pray, just as John taught his disciples"* (Luke 11:1). This verse also reveals to us that the second Elijah, John the Baptist, was a man of prayer, who taught his followers to pray. Prayer was exciting for the early Church; Pentecost was a prayer meeting! The early believers prayed and acted on their praying. Prayer was never a dull routine for them. They learned what Philip Hughes said: "Prayer is a vital pre-requisite for the release and experience of God's power."

The Elijah People and prayer

There are many excellent books on prayer, and how to pray. I am not going to set out a detailed, prescribed way of prayer for the Church to follow; my plea is that the Church prays. The Holy Spirit will guide each expression of the Elijah People to pray in the way that is necessary for their situation and time. It is often said that prayer changes things. That is true, but I think it is more accurate to say that the God who answers prayer changes things. Prayer is not an end in itself; it is prayer prayed in the name of Jesus to the living God that is effective.

However, there is one aspect of prayer that I feel it is important to draw our attention to, since the New Testament specifically refers to the *way* in which Elijah prayed as an example for us to follow. James tells us that Elijah prayed 'earnestly' that it would not rain (James

5:17). The literal reading of this verse says, 'with prayer he prayed'. Elijah prayed in his praying. This way of expressing Elijah's praying was a common idiom of the time to express that he prayed intensely or fervently. Jesus used the same idiom when he said to the disciples, *"I have eagerly desired to eat this Passover with you before I suffer"* (Luke 22:15). Jesus' actual words were, "With desire I have desired to eat..."

The Church prayed for Peter fervently when he was in prison (Acts 12:5). This word means strenuous; it is also used in 1Peter 1:22 where we are urged to love one another fervently (some translations have 'from the heart'). If our praying does not move us, what makes us think it will move God? The way in which we are encouraged to emulate Elijah in prayer, therefore, is to pray earnestly, fervently, strenuously and intensely. This does not mean we whip ourselves into a frenzy like the Baal-Melqart prophets did at Mount Carmel. They screamed and ranted frantically, cutting themselves with swords until their blood flowed. We rightly dismiss such actions as worthless. You cannot convince God to act by crawling around on broken glass in self-humiliation or wearing a hair shirt, real or spiritual. When we pray earnestly we are not trying to convince God to act by harming ourselves or shouting at him at the top of our voices. God is not deaf. Neither is he convinced or persuaded to respond by our acts of self-harm or extreme asceticism. God does not require these pointless deeds of religion to persuade him to act.

We see several examples of Elijah's earnest praying. Let me mention just three of them.

First, when he prayed over the body of the dead boy, he did so three times. When nothing happened the first time he did not stop. When his second prayer did not result in the boy's miracle, Elijah continued. He prayed again a third time. He would have prayed a fourth or fifth if necessary. That boy was coming back to life!

Second, when Elijah prayed on top of Mount Carmel for the rain to fall, he prayed seven times. He had heard from God that it was going to rain and it was time to pray it in. So he prayed until the cloud appeared.

Third, as I mentioned earlier, when God spoke to him at Horeb, Elijah prayed the same prayer twice. This was not vain repetition or mere recital of a religious routine. Elijah came again and again to God in prayer with the burden of his heart. Earnest prayer is not the amount of times we pray about something; it is *how* we pray. Elijah prayed until he knew that his prayer was effective. He prevailed in his prayer. As the Christians of a previous generation used to say: he prayed his prayer through.

We must also note that Jesus prayed like this. During those immense, critical hours before his death he went to the Garden of Gethsemane (which means 'oil press' or 'oil crusher'), where he felt the full pressure of what he was about to undertake in order to save the world from sin. In preparation for the forthcoming hours he prayed to his Father. While Peter, James and John fell asleep, the Gospels record that Jesus prayed three times so intensely that his sweat was like drops of blood falling to the ground and an angel came to strengthen him (Luke 22:43-44). Jesus also gave us examples of how to pray earnestly. He told the parable of the unjust judge and the widow:

Jesus told his disciples a parable to show them that they should always pray and not give up. He said: "In a certain town there was a judge who neither feared God nor cared about men. And there was a widow in that town who kept coming to him with the plea, 'Grant me justice against my adversary.' "For some time he refused. But finally he said to himself, 'Even though I don't fear God or care about men, yet because this widow keeps bothering me, I will see that she gets justice, so that she won't eventually wear me out with her coming!"' (Luke 18:1-5)

Jesus said we must always pray and never give up. We pray in faith and prayer increases our faith. The more we pray the more we believe. God is not unjust; he is good. The point of the parable is that we must be like the widow in the story who kept coming again and again until she received what rightfully was hers: justice. In the same way she bothered the judge (the word 'bothering' actually means to give somebody a black eye!), so we must 'bother' God. We do not threaten or cajole God, shake our fists at him or verbally abuse him; we just keep coming again and again to him in bold and confident faith that he will answer us. We lay hold of God in prayer and do not let go of him until we receive what we are praying for. We pray things through. Jesus also told us to:

"Ask and it will be given to you; seek and you will find; knock and the door will be opened to you. For everyone who asks receives; he who seeks finds; and to him who knocks, the door will be opened." (Matthew 7:7-8)

The structure of this passage indicates continuous asking, continuous seeking and continuous knocking:

we have to keep on asking, keep on seeking and keep on knocking. The kind of prayer established in Elijah that James urges us to emulate is persistent, persevering, unshakeable, constant praying. The prayer of the Elijah People is prayer that never gives up and never gives in. Just as the prophet Isaiah urged us – we give ourselves no rest and we give the Lord no rest until he makes Zion the praise of the earth (Isaiah 62:6-7). The prayers of the Elijah People are prophetic prayers.

In particular, we pray earnestly for the purpose of God to be fulfilled; for the kingdom of God to come in all its fullness; for the maturity of the sons of God; for the souls of men and women to be saved; for the knowledge of the glory of the Lord to cover the earth; for our cities and streets; for our families and friends; for Jesus to have a Church worthy of his name. Jesus said that his house is a house of prayer (Matthew 21:13). That is why he cleared it of all the rubbish and religious paraphernalia that had crept in to take the place of this essential characteristic of his people. As the return of Jesus draws ever nearer the need for the earnest prayers of the Elijah People increases. Let us 'pray in our praying' what Jesus taught us to pray:

Father in heaven. Hallowed be your name. Your kingdom come, your will be done on earth as it is in heaven. (Matthew 6:9-10)

ELEVEN

Back to Basics (1)

"The Israelites have rejected your covenant, broken down your altars, and put your prophets to death with the sword." (1Kings 19:10)

It is said that pressure reveals character; it also reveals what is in a person's heart. Jesus said that out of the overflow of our hearts our mouths speak (Matthew 12:34). What is in our hearts will eventually come out of our mouths. When Elijah was under pressure after fleeing from Jezebel's death threat, his reply to God's searing question – "What are you doing here?" – revealed his heart. It was so deep in his heart that he said exactly the same thing when God asked him the same question a second time. This is what made Elijah tick.

When all was said and done, what really grieved Elijah's heart about the state of his people came out of his mouth in this statement: they had rejected God's covenant; they had broken down God's altars; and they had killed God's prophets. The people of God had sinned in three basic but fundamentally important areas of life. Let us look at each of them and discover how we as the Elijah People live like Elijah in total contrast to our contemporaries. These are three aspects of the restoration of all things.

1. Rejected God's covenant

The subject of covenant demands a book of its own. Covenant is one of the major themes of Scripture, and features all the way from Genesis to Revelation. As such, it is too enormous for me to do it justice within the confines of these pages. What I say about covenant, therefore, will have to suffice to whet the appetite of the reader to investigate this wonderful subject at closer hand.

In its simplest terms a covenant is an agreement, a binding together. The essence of covenant is an agreement in which people enter into a mutual binding relationship concerning something. In ancient times, as it is today, it was used to describe contracts, treaties, marriage, and business transactions. Covenant is all to do with relationship.

In Bible times, when people made covenants, they would often perform a ceremony in which they took animals, killed them and cut them in half. The pieces were laid out and the two people making their covenant would walk together between the pieces, symbolising that they were now one. This walk together was a solemn pledge that if either of them broke the terms of their covenant agreement then what had happened to the animals would happen to them. (See Genesis 15, where God confirmed his covenant with Abraham by doing this). Covenant, then, is a serious matter; in fact, ultimately it is a matter of life and death.

Covenant is the way that God exists. The Trinity itself is a covenant: the Father, Son and Holy Spirit exist as a covenant. John Wesley called the Trinity a 'sweet society'. God is one in three and three in one. God's name Yahweh is said to be the covenant name of God, because every covenant he makes depends on his ability and nature as the unchanging I AM to keep his covenant promise. God binds himself to his covenant promises. If he broke his covenant he would cease to exist. God never acts outside of his covenant nature, plan and purpose. God is the God of covenant. Therefore, covenant is the way he relates not only to himself but also to humanity. He makes and always keeps his covenant with people. When he establishes covenant God establishes relationship, because the heart of covenant is relationship. God's original and ultimate intention is for his people to be a covenant people: in covenant with him and with each other. This is the great theme that runs through all the biblical covenants: God often says, "I will be your God and you will be my people" (Exodus 6:7; Jeremiah 7:23; 30:22). The history of God's people is a history of covenants, which are all part of God's single magnificent purpose, to fill the earth with a people – a covenant family – in his image (Genesis 1:26-27). God joins himself to his people in covenant; he keeps every promise he makes because he is faithful to his covenant. In the Old Testament, God made several major covenants:

• With Adam (Genesis 1:26-29; Hosea 6:7);
• With Noah (Genesis 9:8-15);
• With Abraham (Genesis 15 and 17);
• With Moses and the Israelites (Exodus 19:1-6);
• With David (2Samuel 7).

These Old Testament covenants were each designed by God to be staging posts in his overall purpose. In all his dealings with the people of the Old Testament he was moving towards something even greater, to establishing his everlasting covenant with all who believe in his name. These covenant people come from every people group and nation and are the people of God, filling the whole earth with the knowledge of God's glory.

All the Old Testament covenants are ultimately fulfilled in the New Covenant. This New Covenant is a Person – the Lord Jesus Christ (see Isaiah 42:6-7, Mark 14:24). All the Old Testament covenants are fulfilled in him (Jeremiah 31:31-34). The New Covenant in Jesus Christ is, therefore, the climax of every Old Testament covenant. Indeed, as we have already discussed, the eternal covenant purpose of God was always centred in Jesus Christ right from the very beginning (Genesis 3:15). The New Covenant in Christ is not merely the last and greatest of the covenants: every Old Testament covenant is to do with Jesus. Jesus *is* the New Covenant; he is the ultimate covenant expression of God. As the New Covenant people of God we are joined to him and also to every other believer in the Lord Jesus Christ in a binding covenant relationship of love and faithful loyalty. That is why divisions among Christians and denominational labels that declare our disagreements are such a denial of who we are as the covenant people of God, and more important, a denial of who God is.

No wonder Elijah was grieved by the appalling situation that prevailed among the people of his day. They had rejected their covenant relationship with God, preferring to worship and serve the false god Baal-Melqart. These were God's own people whom he loved and had chosen. They belonged to him and he belonged to them. They were supposed to live according to the covenant agreements and promises that God had made with Abraham, Moses and David. But they had rejected those covenants and in doing so had rejected God himself. In a graphic, prophetic demonstration of this, Elijah restored the altar of the Lord at Mount Carmel in a particular, deliberate way:

> *Elijah took twelve stones, one for each of the tribes descended from Jacob, to whom the word of Yahweh had come, saying, "Your name shall be Israel." With the stones he built an altar in the name of Yahweh. (1Kings 18:31-32)*

Elijah reminded the people who they really were: God's covenant people. They were the descendants of Jacob, whom God had renamed Israel. They were the offspring of Abraham and Isaac, men of the covenant promises of God. Elijah restored the altar with twelve stones: a powerful reminder to them that they had become a divided nation (the ten northern tribes who had separated from the two southern tribes after Solomon's death). Through Elijah's prophetic act, God was calling them back to himself to be his covenant people.

The Church is God's covenant people

The Church as the Elijah People expresses the covenant nature of God; we are, therefore, a covenant people. Pentecost produced a covenant people; and the closing verses of Acts chapter two give us some insights into how these early Elijah People lived out the covenant they had entered with God and each other through their new birth in Jesus:

> *Those who accepted [Peter's] message were baptised, and about three thousand were added to*

their number that day. They devoted themselves to the apostles' teaching and to the fellowship, to the breaking of bread and to prayer. Everyone was filled with awe, and many wonders and miraculous signs were done by the apostles. All the believers were together and had everything in common. Selling their possessions and goods, they gave to anyone as he had need. Every day they continued to meet together in the temple courts. They broke bread in their homes and ate together with glad and sincere hearts, praising God and enjoying the favour of all the people. And the Lord added to their number daily those who were being saved. (Acts 2:41-47)

Let us note some of the characteristics of their covenant life. These are also continuously being restored to the Church in increasing measure, dimension and revelation by each generation of the Elijah People.

A people who accepted the message. Those who accepted the message of the Gospel proved their submission to the Lordship of Jesus by being immediately baptised in water and receiving the gift of the Holy Spirit. They did not try and negotiate the terms of their salvation to suit themselves. Note that the verse speaks of those who accepted Peter's message; that tells me that there were those who did not. Nevertheless, Peter refused to compromise the demands of the Gospel to accommodate people's preferences. He was prepared to allow people to walk away rather than water down the Lordship of Jesus. The message of the Gospel of the Kingdom includes the fact that when we receive Jesus as Lord we become part of God's covenant people.

Added to their number. Prior to Pentecost there already existed an apostolic community of one hundred and twenty believers. The new believers were added to them. They did not get saved and then go off to start their own Church, or decide not to join the Church. They did not begin an alternative Church – the Second Church of Jerusalem – or anything as nonsensical as that. There was only one Church. Before Jesus returns there will come an end to the constant fracturing and division of his Body. Christians speak about Church unity, but rarely speak about covenant as an expression of that unity. There is no true unity outside covenant, because the unity, or oneness, that God speaks about is a covenant unity or oneness. That is the essence of Jesus' prayer to his Father in John 17:20-23. If we as the Elijah People speak more about oneness than unity then we will rediscover much quicker that we are a covenant people.

They devoted themselves. These Christians were devoted, dedicated and committed. They counted the cost and had signed up for the cause of Christ. They were not fair-weather attendees of Church meetings who would flee at the first sign of opposition or hard work. The actual term used here denotes a prevailing persistence, to continue to do something with intense effort and strength. It is a persistence that prevails despite difficulties. For the early Elijah People there was no opt out clause; they were in forever, in good times and bad. Too many modern Christians run for the hills at the first sign of trouble. Others flit from Church to Church, depending on how good the preacher is or how anointed the worship is. People take offence because somebody ignored them in a meeting, and leave the Church with criticism and bitterness. Others see themselves as attenders of services rather than active parts of the Body of Christ, with little or no commitment. The Elijah People of Acts were not like that; they devoted themselves to four things in particular:

(i) Devoted to the apostles' teaching. They lived according to what the apostles taught them. The apostles determined what the Church would believe and practise. Their authenticity as the Church was determined by whether they followed the teaching and doctrine of the apostles. Nobody was his own final authority concerning what he believed; if you wanted to be part of the Church you believed and practised what the apostles taught. This is a massive issue for today. Who determines what you believe? Who has the ultimate authority concerning your faith? It is not good enough to answer that by saying, "God has the final authority." How does God exercise that final authority over you? You cannot say, "The Bible is my final authority." In reality, it is what *you* believe the Bible says that is *your* final authority. So, who decides and determines what *you* believe? According to the New Testament, apostles do. Apostles exist today and they still have that responsibility: they are subject to the Word of God and do not write new Scripture. Nevertheless, they determine what the Church believes. I am aware that this is a radical statement and is one I have considered, studied and written about extensively elsewhere. I do not have the space to pursue it further here, but mention it because it is a question the Church will have to address. All I want to say here is that the current practice among Christians in which each person is ultimately their own final authority is not the biblical norm and will have to change.

(ii) Devoted to the Fellowship. These believers shared a common life (that is what the word *fellowship* means). They shared a common identity and a common purpose. They saw themselves as one people. They believed the same things and identified with each other in all areas of life. This was evidenced in their common life through sharing their homes and possessions. They met each other's needs generously and with no expectation of repayment; they ate together, opening their lives to each other and sharing their food. They were not communists; they were a community, a covenant people. They enjoyed this way of life, sharing the love of Jesus with each other. They were glad, filled with the joy of the Lord. They were sincere; the genuine article. No charge of hypocrisy could be justifiably levelled against them. They viewed themselves as one people, the community of the King.

(iii) Devoted to the breaking of bread. One of the most important things they did was to regularly break bread together. The Lord's Supper or Communion as some call it was not a religious rite for them in which the minister or priest officiated. There were no ministers or priests! It was a covenant meal they ate together – in their homes – in which they remembered what Jesus had done and affirmed their covenant with the Lord and with each other. Jesus had said this meal celebrated the New Covenant in his blood (Mark 14:24). Later, Paul would explain in more detail the corporate nature of the covenant meal (1Corinthians 11); it is a meal to be shared, in which we remind ourselves of our corporate, covenant identity as the people of God. The covenant meal expresses the vertical and horizontal aspects of living as God's covenant people. It is vertical in that we

meet and fellowship the risen and ascended Jesus; it is horizontal in that we eat in fellowship with our covenant brothers and sisters.

(iv) Devoted to prayer. As we have already discussed, prayer was their vital breath. Prayer permeated their whole covenant life together.

We should not be surprised that such a Church as we read about in Acts saw miracles, signs and wonders on a regular basis; that praise was a hallmark; that they enjoyed the favour of their non-Christian friends and neighbours; and that they grew rapidly in numbers every day. The Lord added to them. After all, as the Psalm said:

> *How good and pleasant it is when brothers dwell together in unity... there Yahweh bestows his blessing, even life for evermore. (Psalm 133:1,3)*

2. Broken down God's altars

The second thing that broke Elijah's heart concerning God's covenant people was that they had broken down God's altars. The Bible contains almost four hundred references to altars; they are highly significant, as the *Dictionary of Biblical Imagery* indicates:

> *Nothing is more prominent as a biblical image for worship...the most visible sign of one's true to devotion to God in the old covenant is the building of, or travelling to, altars for acts of sacrifice and offering.*

In the Bible, altars fundamentally are all to do with worship, and in particular, worship expressed in sacrifice. The first person to build an altar in Scripture was Noah, after the Flood:

Noah built an altar to Yahweh and, taking some of all the clean animals and clean birds, he sacrificed burnt offerings on it. (Genesis 8:20)

The first explicit mention of worship in the Bible occurs when God tested Abraham's faith and obedience, by commanding him to build an altar and sacrifice his son Isaac as a burnt offering on it (see Genesis 22). Immediately Abraham obeyed God and set off with Isaac for the place God had told him to perform the sacrifice. For Abraham, the sacrifice of Isaac on the altar he would build was an act of worship to God:

On the third day Abraham looked up and saw the place in the distance. He said to his servants, "Stay here with the donkey while I and the boy go over there. We will worship and then we will come back to you." (Genesis 22:4-5)

Increasingly in the Old Testament we see the institution by God of the various sacrifices and offerings that people offered to him at the altar of the Tabernacle and later in the Temple at Jerusalem. We do not have the time to discuss these in detail; however it needs to be closely noted that this worship of God at the altar more often than not involved the blood sacrifice of animals. The Hebrew word for *altar* comes from a word meaning *slaughter*. Of course, as the New Testament tells us, and the letter to the Hebrews in particular, the whole sacrificial system of the Old Testament – priests, sacrifice and altar – are all fulfilled in Jesus, in who he is, what he has done, and what he does now. Jesus is the priest, the sacrifice and the altar:

> *Since we have a great high priest who has gone through the heavens, Jesus the Son of God, let us hold firmly to the faith we profess. (Hebrews 4:14)*

> *Since we have confidence to enter the Most Holy Place by the blood of Jesus, by a new and living way opened for us through the curtain, that is, his body, and since we have a great priest over the house of God, let us draw near to God with a sincere heart in full assurance of faith. (Hebrews 10:19-22)*

> *We have an altar from which those who minister at the tabernacle have no right to eat. (Hebrews 13:10)*

At Mount Carmel, Elijah restored the altar of the Lord, which had gone to ruin (1Kings 18:30). The fire from heaven came down on the sacrifice that was placed on the restored altar of twelve stones, which signify God's covenant. The covenant people of God are the true worshippers of God. The Elijah People are first and foremost worshippers of God:

> *Therefore, I urge you, brothers, in view of God's mercy, to offer your bodies as living sacrifices, holy and pleasing to God—this is your spiritual act of worship [literally: your rational or logical service]. (Romans 12:1)*

God the Father seeks a certain kind of people – worshippers. These people worship him in Spirit and in truth (John 4:21-24). Worship is at the centre of Christianity – it is the core. Christians are, before anything else, worshippers of Jesus. As the story of Elijah so graphically demonstrates to us, the question we all have to answer is: 'Who or what do I worship?' Whatever or whoever has the prior place in my life; whatever I value the most; the most precious thing to me is what I worship. Worship is not just something I do in a Church meeting where we have 'a time of worship'; worship is the kind of person I am. Tony Ling wrote:

> *True worship is not singing songs, clapping, and raising hands in the presence of God. True worship is not shouting and jumping. It may include all those things, but true worship is laying down your life for God.... Worship is giving myself utterly, totally, unconditionally to God.*

Romans 12 says that we offer ourselves as living sacrifices in worship. Sometimes I hear people say things like, "I don't want to worship the Lord, but I'm willing to make the sacrifice." "Worship was a real sacrifice for me today – I am wearing a new suit and I had to kneel before the Lord." "I'm not the worshipping kind." "Do I have to raise my hands?" As Tozer said, "If worship bores you, you are not ready for heaven." Sacrifice is not going without things or creature comforts; it is not some kind of spiritual self-denial. Sacrificial worship means giving yourself completely in abandoned love and adoration to Jesus. It is a way of life, not something you do for thirty minutes on a Sunday or when you attend a 'worship conference'.

Worship is all about who or what we value the most. Psalm 115:8 says we become like who or what we worship. Practically, we worship the things we talk about the most; what excites and motivates us the most; what we spend most of our time and energy on; where we spend our money the most; what we love the most. Anything and anybody can become the object of our worship. For the Elijah People, nothing can replace or supplant the preeminence and centrality of Jesus. This does not mean that we are forbidden to enjoy life and involve ourselves in other things: sport, movies, career, hobbies, family, fashion, cars, for example. Personally, I am an avid cricket fan and am passionate about Welsh rugby! I enjoy good food and holidays in the sun. We are not narrow-minded killjoys; the Elijah People love life. Nevertheless, the centre and circumference of our life is Jesus; and the reason we live is to worship him.

3. Put God's prophets to death

The third thing that broke Elijah's heart was that God's covenant people had put God's prophets to death. They had allowed Jezebel to carry out her campaign of terror and the murder of God's spokesmen. Elijah was left distraught both by the tragic deaths of those he probably knew personally, and by the fact that God's voice was being silenced. The nation had done away with, or so it thought, the Word of God. In killing the prophets, Jezebel hoped to quash God's voice. God's Word is God's voice.

I will deal with this third aspect of Elijah's concern only briefly, since we have already discussed at length the relationship of the Elijah People to the Word of God. Let me just take the opportunity here to reiterate and re-emphasise our commitment to upholding the integrity and authority of the Word of God, the Bible. Not only that: we as the Elijah People align our lives completely with the Bible and the God of the Bible. That inevitably means we live out of step with the world and with those religious, so-called Christian institutions and organisations (I refuse to call them the Church) who deny and erode the truth of the Scriptures. We choose to live against the tide of popular opinion and current, passing fancies that play with fire in diminishing and denigrating God's eternal Word.

Furthermore, as we have previously said, we as the Elijah People speak the Word of God to our world and to the Church that needs to be restored. We speak confrontation when and where necessary; we encourage with words of commendation; we speak the word of hope. We speak the creative and prophetic Word of God, calling into being what the Church has yet to be in the restoration purpose of God. Our words are the words of the living God, who cannot be silenced. The world may kill the messengers of the Word, but the Word itself is eternal and indestructible. It can never be put to death: it is the Word of the living God.

TWELVE

Back to Basics (2)

Gilgal...Bethel...Jericho...Jordan (2Kings 2)

Elijah spent his last day on earth taking his prophetic successor Elisha on a tour. This was no farewell trip or a nostalgic last look at some famous sights; Elijah had a specific purpose in what he did during those final hours. He took Elisha to four places that had played a vital role in forming the identity and destiny of God's covenant people. Elijah gave Elisha the final preparation he needed for his ministry. He took him back to his roots, back to basics. These places serve as reminders for us as the Elijah People too, of who we are in Christ, of what the Lord has done for us; and what his purpose is for us. In this brief chapter, I will highlight the significance of each location for us as the Elijah People. In moving forward to maturity it is imperative that we do not forsake or neglect what is already restored. We never abandon covenant, for example; we take it with us and its significance for us in God's restoration purpose continually increases.

Gilgal

Gilgal was the place where the new generation of Israelites under Joshua's leadership first camped after crossing the Jordan (Joshua 4:19). Several important things happened to them here. First, they set up a covenant memorial comprising the twelve stones they had miraculously taken from the dry riverbed as they crossed over. This covenant memorial was to serve as a constant reminder to the future generations of what the Lord had done for his people, and so that: *All the peoples of the earth might know that the hand of Yahweh is powerful and so that you might always fear Yahweh your God* (Joshua 4:24). It also acted as a sign and active remembrance that God's people are a covenant people. It was the first thing they did at Gilgal; this demonstrates the centrality of covenant for the Elijah People.

At Gilgal the new generation was also circumcised. The word '*Gilgal*' means *roll away* and derives from what their circumcision achieved that important day: *Yahweh said to Joshua, "Today I have rolled away the reproach of Egypt from you." So the place has been called Gilgal to this day* (Joshua 5:9). Circumcision was the Old Testament sign of covenant, of belonging, of identity. In the New Testament circumcision is spiritual, a circumcision of the heart (Romans 2:29), the removal of the old sinful nature and the new birth. Circumcision of the heart is proved in water baptism (Colossians 2:11-12). In baptism we are baptised into Jesus and into his Body.

Gilgal was the place where they ate their first Passover in the promised land (Joshua 5:10-12). It was also where the very next day the manna they had eaten every day for forty years in the desert finally ceased. Gilgal was the place where the old had gone and the new had come (2Corinthians 5:17).

We as the Elijah People live in the power of the Lord in the fear of the Lord; we live in the truth of who we are as new creations in Christ, free from the curse and reproach of sin (*Egypt* is often depicted as the old sinful life); we live in the good of all that Jesus, the Passover Lamb, has achieved for us. These are our *'Gilgals'* – constant reminders for us to spur us on in faith as the covenant people of God.

Bethel

Bethel means *house of God*. Its first mention is in Genesis 12:8. Abraham camped there soon after his arrival in Canaan. At Bethel he built an altar to Yahweh and called on the name of Yahweh. For Abraham, Bethel was the place of worship and prayer, and of the manifest presence of God. He returned to Bethel after his time in Egypt, and again he called on the name of Yahweh there.

At Bethel, Abraham's grandson Jacob had his first encounter with God, when he saw in a dream the stairway of God with angels ascending and descending on it. To his shame Jacob did not realise he was in the presence of God, saying, *"Surely, Yahweh is in this place and I was not aware of it"* (Genesis 28:16). He heard the voice of God for the first time at Bethel:

"I am Yahweh, the God of your father Abraham and the God of Isaac. I will give you and your offspring the land on which you are lying." (Genesis 28:13)

Years later God told Jacob, now called Israel, to settle in Bethel and build an altar there (Genesis 35:1-14). Jacob did so and called the place El Bethel (*'God of the house of God'*). Elijah took Elisha to Bethel on that fateful day to remind him that God's people are God's house, God's dwelling place, a people of worship, prayer, and the presence of God. We saw earlier that Jesus burned with zeal for God's house and that the house of God is a heavenly, spiritual house. Bethel serves as a constant reminder that we as the Elijah People are God's house, a people of worship, of prayer and of his heavenly presence. The distinguishing mark of the Church as the Elijah People is the manifest, tangible presence of God among us. We live for the honour and glory of God's house, and his presence is the distinctive feature that marks us as his unique people.

Jericho

At Jericho, the new generation of Israelites had their first victory after crossing Jordan (Joshua 6). Jericho was a major city that stood in their way; it was an imposing obstacle that they could not avoid or go around. They had to defeat Jericho in order to progress to the conquest of the rest of Canaan. They had to overcome and defeat their enemy. Their victory was achieved supernaturally: for six days they marched around Jericho once each day. Then on the seventh day they marched around seven times. On each occasion they were commanded not to utter a sound. However, on the seventh time on the seventh day they were ordered to shout and the walls of Jericho fell to the ground in a heap. After the victory Joshua stood over the defeated city and spoke the Word of the Lord:

> "Cursed before Yahweh is the man who undertakes to rebuild this city, Jericho: At the cost of his firstborn son will he lay its foundations; at the cost of his youngest will he set up its gates."
> (Joshua 6:26)

Hundreds of years later – ironically in the time of Ahab and Jezebel – a man named Hiel (from Bethel of all places) did a foolish thing:

In Ahab's time, Hiel of Bethel rebuilt Jericho. He laid its foundations at the cost of his firstborn son Abiram, and he set up its gates at the cost of his youngest son Segub, in accordance with the word of Yahweh spoken by Joshua son of Nun. (1 Kings 16:34)

Jericho reminded Elisha that the God of Elijah is the living God who reigns in victory and with all authority, and whose word is eternally powerful. As God had been with Elijah so he would be with Elisha. Jericho reminds us that Jesus has won a great victory over Satan, whom he has utterly defeated. We live in the reality of that victory. Jesus has conquered all his enemies – sin, sickness and death – and he reigns supreme as the King of kings and Lord of lords. Even though the enemy might come against us to try and destroy us, the power of God's word is always mighty to destroy and frustrate his plans. Just like the word of the Lord that Joshua spoke lived on after his death, so the victory that Jesus achieved when he crushed Satan's head at Golgotha, the Place of the Skull, is just as effective today. As the Elijah People we live in the present in the good of the past and in the light of the future. That is why Paul could say with faith and in complete confidence:

In all these things we win an overwhelming victory. We keep on gloriously conquering. We overwhelmingly overcome; we are more than conquerors through him who loves us. (Romans 8:37)

Jordan

The Jordan River signifies the crossing over from one life to another. The natural river was the barrier or boundary between the eastern desert region and the fertile land to the west. It was a boundary between two kinds of life: a hard life working the desert soil, and the life of abundance drawn from the rich soil to the west of the river. Ironically, Elijah's forebears had decided that they preferred to remain on the east of Jordan, rather than enter into the blessings of what lay beyond Jordan. Elijah himself would not be bound or limited by his past; he had moved on from it many years previously in order to fulfil his destiny.

When Israel crossed over from the east to the west they did so miraculously (Joshua 3:15-17). The water stopped flowing as soon as they reached the water's edge and the people crossed over on dry land. Their departure from one way of life and entry into another was a miracle. The river marked the boundary between the two. And once they had crossed over, the river returned to its normal flow. There was no way back; the past was gone; only the hope-filled, glorious, abundant future lay ahead. They were being restored!

For us the Jordan is a constant reminder that we have passed from death to life and there is no return to the old sinful past. We have passed through into the life of abundance and blessing in Christ, and a glorious inheritance. The Lord has marked a boundary between the way we used to live and the way we live now as his Elijah People. Just as the Israelites were intended to fill the new land with the presence and covenant life of God, so we are the means by which the Holy Spirit fills the earth with the knowledge of the glory of the Lord as the waters cover the sea. Jordan for us marks the beginning of the life of restoration, and as we move forward into the life of the Spirit we grow from glory to glory, constantly being restored to mature sonship.

Constant reminders

So we see that Elijah's purpose with Elisha in taking him to these four locations was to leave with him active reminders of the God Elisha served, what God had done for his people, and the kind of people God wanted. These are also four 'locations' in our lives as the Elijah People. We always live in the good of what Gilgal, Bethel, Jericho and Jordan represent for us. They act as reminders and markers to encourage us, provoke us and to build us up as we give ourselves to the restoration purpose of God. We must never forget nor forsake them; they are living truths for us every moment of our lives.

THIRTEEN

Forerunners

Prepare the way of the Lord. (John 1:23)

Elijah was a forerunner. He prepared the way for the one who would come after him: the prophet Elisha. When Elijah experienced his own restoration after fleeing in fear from Jezebel, God instructed him: *"Anoint Elisha son of Shaphat from Abel Meholah to succeed you as prophet"* (1Kings 19:16).

Remember: Elisha did not succeed Elijah because of Elijah's failure. We established that the latter part of his life was more powerful and significant than the early part. Rather, this is the compensation principle of restoration at work again. If you take time to read the story of Elisha's ministry in the second book of Kings, you will discover that he had a greater measure than Elijah, achieved far more than Elijah, and completed many of the things that Elijah had started. An interesting example of the greater magnitude of Elisha is found in 2Kings 13:20-22:

Elisha died and was buried. Now Moabite raiders used to enter the country every spring. Once while some Israelites were burying a man, suddenly they saw a band of raiders; so they threw the man's body into Elisha's tomb. When the body touched

Elisha's bones, the man came to life and stood up on his feet.

Like Elijah, Elisha too raised somebody – a child – from the dead (2Kings 4:18-37). Now, even after his death, when a dead body touched his bones, the man sprang to life again! This story demonstrates to us the compensation element of restoration: even in death Elisha was able to bring life.

This idea of the forerunner preparing the way for the one to come after them is not confined to Elijah and Elisha. We also see it in the example of Moses and Joshua. Moses, who led the Israelites out of their captivity in Egypt, was succeeded by Joshua, who took them into the promised land of Canaan. Joshua led the people where Moses could not. Moses prepared the people for the one who would come after him – Joshua – to take the people into their destiny. It was through Joshua that the people entered the land, defeated their enemies and gained their promised inheritance.

The names Joshua and Elisha both mean *God saves* and are Hebrew forms of the name Jesus. They are both what are commonly called *types* or *shadows* of Jesus: Old Testament examples or illustrations that tell us something about who Jesus is and what he has done. (Colossians 2:16-17 and Hebrews 4:8-11 speak about the Old Testament Sabbath, which means 'rest', as an example of how Jesus has brought us into the rest of God through our salvation. So the Sabbath is a type or shadow of Jesus). Of course, Joshua and Elisha were real men; this principle of types and shadows just means we can glean things from their lives that are revealed fully in the New Testament. In this example of their names we see that Gabriel told Joseph, Mary's husband: *"You are to give him the name Jesus, because he will save his people from their sins"* (Matthew 1:21).

John the Baptist, the second Elijah, specifically described himself as a forerunner; that is why he came. When he was asked he who was, John replied: *"I am the voice of one calling in the desert, 'Make straight the way for the Lord"'* (John 1:23). Each of the other three Gospels (see Matthew 3:3; Mark 1:2-3; Luke 3:4-6) also record the fact that John the Baptist was the forerunner, quoting as John did here, the prophet Isaiah:

> *A voice of one calling: "In the desert prepare the way for Yahweh; make straight in the wilderness a highway for our God. Every valley shall be raised up, every mountain and hill made low; the rough ground shall become level, the rugged places a plain. And the glory of Yahweh will be revealed, and all mankind together will see it. For the mouth of Yahweh has spoken." (Isaiah 40:3-5)*

Gabriel had told John's father Zechariah that his son would *'make ready a people prepared for the Lord'* (Luke 1:17). Remember in an earlier chapter I emphasised that John always identified himself and his ministry in relation to Jesus: *"I am not the Christ, but I have been sent before him" (John 3:28)*. Furthermore, John himself constantly directed people beyond himself to the One who would come after him – Jesus:

> *"After me will come one who is more powerful than I, whose sandals I am not fit to carry." (Matthew 3:11)*

The next day John was there again with two of his disciples. When he saw Jesus passing by, he said, "Look, the Lamb of God!" When the two disciples heard him say this, they followed Jesus. (John 1:35-37)

"He must increase, but I must decrease." (John 3:30)

John understood that his significance in this world was not centred on himself and his own destiny. As the second Elijah his sole purpose was to prepare the way for the launch of the earthly, public ministry of Jesus; to announce to the world that the Word was made flesh; that God was here in the Person of his Son; to direct people towards Jesus, the Lamb of God; and to promote the interests and plan of Jesus. That is why Jesus said of him that nobody up to that time was greater than John the Baptist (Matthew 11:11): his life and ministry had a history-shaping effect and result – he prepared the way for the Lamb of God, the Baptiser in the Spirit, to come and begin the ministry that would save the world from sin. Forerunners, therefore, prepare the way for something incredibly significant. Remember that the Elijah People are greater than John. Jesus said of us: *"He who is least in the kingdom of heaven is greater than he"* (Matthew 11:11).

As the Elijah who is coming, who will restore all things, the result of the Elijah People's life and ministry will be nothing less than the return of the Lord Jesus Christ in glory in his Second Coming. Like Elijah and John the Baptist, we are forerunners, preparers of the way. There is no other Elijah to come; it is we, the Church, who are the third and final manifestation. It is we who will grow to maturity as the sons of God, it is we who will restore all things, it is we who will hasten Jesus' coming (2Peter 3:12). Therefore, it is important that we, the Church as the Elijah People, keep our eyes fixed on the prize. It is all too easy in the day-to-day business of life to lose the focus of our purpose: we are forerunners, preparing the way for Jesus to come again. However, we must not be like the disciples who watched Jesus ascend to heaven:

They were looking intently up into the sky as he was going, when suddenly two men dressed in white stood beside them. "Men of Galilee," they said, "why do you stand here looking into the sky? This same Jesus, who has been taken from you into heaven, will come back in the same way you have seen him go into heaven." (Acts 1:10-11)

We cannot and must not spend all our time gawping, wondering and calculating when Jesus will return. We are not to be spiritual stargazers. He will come when all things spoken by the prophets are restored. We await his coming with anticipation and excitement; but we have a mandate to complete and a maturity to achieve. In all that we do, our focus must be on finishing, keeping everything within the perspective of God's original and ultimate intention: to fill the earth with a covenant family of mature sons who are like their Lord and elder brother: the Father's Eternal Son, Jesus.

The Cost
In conclusion, let me say this: there is an enormous personal cost involved when one belongs to the Elijah

People. Elijah himself had many enemies and intense opposition. He sometimes stood alone as the prophet of God, while those he confronted tried to destroy him. His integrity and character were impugned; his words were twisted and questioned; his life was constantly in danger. He was persecuted and was the object of misunderstanding, scorn and raw hatred. Elijah lived under the conviction of his own word and was affected by it. After his declaration that no rain would fall until he said so, he went to live by the brook Kerith (1Kings 17:5-7). Eventually the brook dried up because of the word that Elijah himself had spoken. He did not live outside of the scope or effect of what he prophesied and preached to others. He, too, was affected by it. Even though Elijah got frightened and feared for his life, ultimately he was a brave man who was willing to pay the price of being identified with God and God's purpose. He persevered and overcame, and ended his time on earth in glory.

John the Baptist too paid a massive price for his revelation of God's purpose and his identity as the second Elijah. In fact, he paid the ultimate price: he was imprisoned and murdered. Like Elijah, John sometimes had questions and times of difficulty and personal crises. When he was languishing in prison he sent disciples to Jesus just to make sure that all he had given his life to was worth it (Matthew 11:2-6). But he died in faith, having fulfilled all he was destined for. John knew that standing against the religious and political powers would endanger his life; he was prepared to pay the cost. He too left this earth in glory. John the Baptist was one of the greatest men who ever lived; yet as we have already discovered, each one of us as the Elijah People is greater than him. We must also be prepared to pay the price he and Elijah paid for their greatness. J.C. Ryle said: "A cheap Christianity that offends nobody, requires no sacrifice and costs nothing is worth nothing."

The early Church and the apostles all suffered persecution in various forms, from insults to death. As the saying goes, it comes with the territory. For many believers in the world today, merely to be identified with Jesus means social ostracism, physical violence or death. In some countries, to be baptised in water as a disciple of Jesus will put your life in danger. In other nations, if you share your faith in Jesus with anybody or gather together as the Church, you will be imprisoned. I read a report recently that estimates up to one hundred thousand Christians a year are martyred for their faith in Jesus. As I write these words I am aware of Christian leaders currently on trial for their lives because they refuse to deny their Lord and Saviour. The charge against them is simply that they have ceased to be Muslims, Hindus, Buddhists or Communists, and have submitted themselves to Jesus. These men and women are our covenant brothers and sisters; they are the Elijah People.

I live in Wales, where none of these things happens. I am grateful to God for that and appreciate what my brothers and sisters in other parts of the world have to bear. I have personal friends who live in other nations and who regularly experience the suffering and persecution I have described. I have had the enormous privilege of visiting some of these countries and seen their suffering for myself. They are my heroes.

Wherever we live in the world as the Elijah People, there will inevitably be varying degrees of opposition, rejection, hatred, misunderstanding, and persecution. The very nature of the Church, as it stands as the agent of the kingdom of God in complete contrast to the kingdoms of this world, increasingly means conflict with the world. This conflict will not always come from political sources alone, but also from religious ones, those systems and structures who wish to retain their status quo and are threatened by the forerunners of the coming Christ. It will even come from those who call themselves Christians: even today I know of situations where 'Churches' that have been approved by atheist governments work with those governments in suppressing true believers, who have to meet in secret places. We are in good company: Jesus experienced the same from the religious leaders of his day. Bryn Jones observed that:

Jesus constantly challenged attitudes that obscured the heart of God, and in the process, he forced legalists to show themselves for what they were. Walking with his disciples through the cornfields on the Sabbath, knowing that they would eat from the corn (Luke 6:1); healing on the Sabbath day with full knowledge that it would offend the priests (Matthew 12:11-12); prophesying the destruction of the temple from its own steps and then speaking of rebuilding it in three days, knowing that they would not understand that he was speaking of his own body in death and resurrection (Matthew 26:61) - all these provocative actions were undertaken with the full awareness that they would provoke angry, inflexible, legalistic responses from the religious hierarchy.

This conflict between the Elijah People and the religious powers, along with their associated political systems that hate or belittle us will vary from disdain and ridicule to slander and direct opposition. It may not be the most severe persecution, but other so-called Christians (from institutionalised, denominationally biased entities) have, in the past, accused the Church to which I belong of being a cult. When I examine their own doctrinal beliefs I wonder how they can even call themselves Christian! We must not be surprised at this; it is only the response of the enemy of our faith as he sees the sons of God growing to maturity and his own eternal destiny in the lake of fire drawing closer. Paul spoke of the inevitable suffering of the Elijah People:

All that belongs to Jesus will belong to us too, if we are prepared to share in his sufferings in order that we may also share in his glory. (Romans 8:17)

The price is worth paying. To be part of the Elijah People is the greatest privilege God can give you, but it will cost you everything. Saul of Tarsus had everything he could possibly want, until he met Jesus:

Whatever was to my profit I now consider loss for the sake of Christ. What is more, I consider everything a loss compared to the surpassing greatness of knowing Christ Jesus my Lord, for whose sake I have lost all things. I consider them excrement, dung, that I may gain Christ. (Philippians 3:7-8)

Let me encourage you: do not give your life for anything that is not worth your life. It is excrement compared to knowing Jesus. God has called you to be part of his Elijah People; he has designed and destined you to play your unique role in his eternal purpose in Christ. I am privileged to be part of such a people; a people who will restore all things and see the return of Jesus in glory! I leave you with this:

If you would make the greatest success of your life, discover what God is doing in your time, and fling yourself into the accomplishment of His purpose and will. (Arthur Wallis)

Further Reading

Roger Aubrey: Apostles Today: an ecclesiological inquiry in the light of the emergence of the New Apostolic Reformation groups, PhD thesis, Cardiff University, UK, 2002

Roger Aubrey: Discovering God, Xulon Press, 2008

Ern Baxter: The King, The Kingdom and the Holy Spirit, Destiny Image, 1995

E.H. Broadbent: The Pilgrim Church, Pickering & Inglis, 1955

Elisabeth Elliot: Through Gates of Splendour, Hodder & Stoughton, 1957

DeVern Fromke: The Ultimate Intention, Sure Foundation, 1998

Bryn Jones: The Radical Church, Destiny Image, 1999

E. Stanley Jones: The Unshakable Kingdom and the Unchanging Person, McNett Press, 1995

E.W. Kenyon: The Father and His Family, Kenyon's Gospel Publishing Society, 1998

Tony Ling: The Lion and the Lamb (Volumes 1&2), Destiny Image, 2006

Watchman Nee: Sit, Walk, Stand, CLC, 1957

Leland Ryken (et al; General Editors): Dictionary of Biblical Imagery, IVP, 1998

Francis Schaeffer: The Church Before the Watching World, IVP, 1972

Francis Schaeffer: The God Who is There, Hodder & Stoughton, 1968

Howard Snyder, The Community of the King, IVP, 1978

T. Austin-Sparks, God's Spiritual House, Tulsa, undated

A.W. Tozer: The Pursuit of God, STL, 1981

Leonard Verduin: The Reformers and Their Stepchildren, Eerdmans, 1964

Arthur Wallis: In the Day of Thy Power, CLC, 1961

Arthur Wallis: The Radical Christian, Kingsway, 1981

Christopher Wright: The Mission of God, IVP, 2006